Burn, Baby! BURN!

Music in American Life

*A list of books in the series appears
at the end of this book.*

Burn, Baby! BURN!

The Autobiography of
Magnificent Montague

**Magnificent Montague
with Bob Baker**

UNIVERSITY OF ILLINOIS PRESS
URBANA AND CHICAGO

∞ This book is printed on acid-free paper.

Library of Congress Cataloging-in-Publication Data
Montague, Nathaniel, 1928–
Burn, baby! burn! : the autobiography of Magnificent
Montague / Magnificent Montague with Bob Baker.
p.   cm. — (Music in American life)
Includes bibliographical references (p.) and index.
ISBN 0-252-02873-2 (cloth : alk. paper)
1. Montague, Nathaniel, 1928– .
2. Disc jockeys—United States—Biography.
3. African Americans—Biography.
I. Baker, Bob, 1947– .
II. Title.
III. Series.
ML429.M68A3   2003
791.44'3—dc21   2003002473

From Montague to Rose and Martin, and from Bob to Marjorie and Amanda. Thanks for sharing the families' quality time on our epic.

A special acknowledgment to Montague's matchless, dearest friend, Allen Klein of ABKCO Records, without whose support this book would have remained an unheard melody.

I have faith in my people.
I wish to exalt them.
I want their lives snatched
from obscurity.

—Rev. William J. Simmons,
 *Men of Mark: Eminent,
 Progressive and Rising* (1887)

Contents

Illustrations follow pages 50 and 122

Introduction

BOB BAKER

This autobiography of Magnificent Montague started in my twelfth-grade chemistry class, thirty-eight years ago.

The kid next to me was telling the kid next to him about a disc jockey—a *black* disc jockey—who was screaming like a man possessed, playing all these great rhythm-and-blues songs that the white stations never played. This was the fall of 1965, and to a white boy at a San Fernando Valley high school where maybe three of the three thousand students were black, this was extremely hip information. "Montague!" one of the boys kept saying. "You gotta hear Montague!"

I tuned in the station the next morning before school—KGFJ, 1230 on the AM dial, a distant journey from 930 and "Boss Radio," the carefully formatted home of the Beatles and Beach Boys—and there it was, this dynamic parallel universe full of people I'd never heard of, like B. B. King and Johnnie Taylor and J. J. Jackson. It was full of rough, hidden classics by black artists whose full brilliance never crossed over to white radio: Otis Redding's "Mister Pitiful" or the Contours' "First I Look at the Purse," which I still remember giggling at the first time I heard it ("If the purse is fat / that's where it's at!"). Before that day, about the only black music I had heard was the more tepid sounds of Motown or Brook Benton or Dinah Washington or the country-and-western style of Ray Charles. But what really froze me with delight was Magnificent Montague himself. He was feverishly shouting or screaming, like he thought he was one of the artists—and damned if he wasn't.

There was real-life drama here. Coming in as a listener shortly after the Watts riots, I was able to infer that Montague had previously used a favorite expression, one that the listeners would call in and scream: "Burn, baby! Burn!" This urgent and mysterious subculture pulled me along with anticipation. What was Montague going to do on the air today? What were his callers going to bring to the table? It felt like the show was the most important thing in his life, and as a result, it became the most important thing in my bleak social existence. It made me want to wake up in the morning.

A few months after I started listening to Montague, I graduated from high school and started attending a state college just down the street from home. I would sit in my parents' 1959 Rambler station wagon a half-hour before class, transfixed by the show. There were 25,000 students on that campus the year I showed up, 98 percent of them white. I had no friends there that first semester, and I did not know anyone who listened to what I was hearing. It was mine, mine alone—for about a year and a half. Then, in the spring of 1967, Montague left KGFJ for whereabouts unknown. I stopped listening. I probably would have anyway: one afternoon around that time, I heard both Jimi Hendrix and the protest singer Phil Ochs for the first time at a friend's apartment, and soul music's lure began to fade.

I graduated from college and became a newspaper reporter. In the early seventies Montague showed up again briefly on a station broadcasting from Mexico, working with Wolfman Jack. As I recall, that gig lasted a year or so, and then Montague faded completely into a romantic memory, something that, on the occasions I pondered it, made me wonder whether he could have been as magnificent as I remembered.

Bruce Springsteen was the most important guy in my world in 1985 when I realized the twentieth anniversary of the Watts riots was approaching. I was a reporter at the *Los Angeles Times* trying to think of an anniversary idea, and "What happened to . . ." popped into my head. I walked over to my city editor and started telling him about this crazy deejay who had coined "Burn, baby! Burn!" on the radio before the riots. It was all news to my boss. Sure, he said, tell the story.

I called KGFJ and got lucky. The veteran station exec who answered the phone had worked with Montague and knew where he was: on the air in Palm Springs. I called Montague and explained that I was an authentic former fan, now armed with the capacity to tell his whereabouts to a million newspaper readers.

"I'm not interested," he said. "Don't like to talk about the past." Eventually he budged and invited me to drive to Palm Springs. There's a moment near the end of *American Graffiti* when Richard Dreyfuss's character finally meets the town's popular deejay, played by Wolfman Jack, and realizes that he is not a black man but rather a pudgy Popsicle-licking white guy. Montague was black, all right, but what stunned me, in much the same way as that movie scene, was his slight build; he was a slender guy standing maybe five feet, five inches tall. How could that booming sound have come out of this man?

Twenty years later it still pained Montague to confront the way "Burn, baby! Burn!" had become the theme song of the Watts riots and so many other subsequent societal outbursts. It was, he tried to tell me, the perversion of something perfect that had transpired spontaneously between him and his listeners. "The words didn't make them burn," he said cautiously. "The words were already there. I just put together the melody."

Gradually he warmed up, until it started to pour out of him. I had to understand how he came up, he said, how hard he had to work, how he learned to sell ads on radio and then to sell himself. How he learned to become as large as the artist whose record he was playing. "Burn, baby! Burn!" he said, "meant that when I'm playing the record and I am snapping my fingers and I'm talking my talk, I have reached the epitome, the height—there is no more you can do!" His words came faster. "Everything is up, up, up! And that's when"—he momentarily softened his voice for drama— "you *burn,* baby—burn. It is like the high five. You know you've hit your home run. There's no more to say. You look at the ball go, like Reggie Jackson. And when I hit that record and I say, 'Darling, I love you,' or 'Put your hand on the radio and touch my heart,' bop-bop-bop BURN, baby! Burn—there was no more to say! That was the epitome! That was it!"

A few years after the article ran, I got another call from Montague. He had sold his radio station and moved back to Los Angeles, he explained, and wondered whether I would take a look at his collection.

Collection of what, I asked?

Books, he said. Paintings. Pamphlets. Movie posters. Engravings. Black. It's all black.

I drove over to his apartment, and he told me how he had fallen in love with collecting African American memorabilia. He told me that he had thousands of pieces in a warehouse in El Monte, a suburb of Los Angeles. He wanted me to help him find a way to turn it into a black history museum.

I was confused. Why would a man whose persona was clearly built on living for the moment turn into a history collector? I didn't realize how long he had been doing this. I wrote another story, and my newspaper published it.

A few years after that Montague called me again, and our conversations led to the notion that perhaps the two sides of his life could be a book. In 1992 we started a series of intermittent interviews spanning several years, interrupted by his radio consulting

jobs, my reporting and editing work, and several unfulfilling encounters with a publishing industry that wanted an easily catego-
rizable autobiography. This infuriated Montague. "I am not simply a deejay!" he would say. The book you now hold in your hands
testifies to that. It spits in the face of the marketing niches that
make popular culture so sterile. It tells the story of a complicated
man who is both fiercely proud of the little-known accomplishments of his race and disdainful of a society that has attempted to
define him by limiting him to a racial box. Montague wants you
to know him as more than a black man—or a deejay. The longer
we worked on the manuscript, the more both of us understood
what the book should sound like. It should sound like his show on
KGFJ, or on WWRL in New York before that, or on WAAF in Chicago before that: a long on-air rap about the glory of music and the
glory of tracking down historical achievement.

Montague's recollections swooped from era to era, creating fragments of a monologue that I eventually glued together. I began
supplementing his stories with research on the personalities whose
paths he crossed. I was fortunate in that Montague, like all collectors, was a pack rat. He still had a printed Paul Robeson speech from
a half-century ago. He still had a poster advertising one of his huge
New York soul concerts from four decades earlier. He still had a tape
of an intimate on-air conversation with Sam Cooke. He still had the
surrealistic novel he had written in the early sixties about a black
boy's encounter with scores of legendary black achievers.

Montague moved to Las Vegas in the midnineties, so we began
conducting our collaboration largely by telephone. For several years
he grew more interested in turning his collection into a Los Angeles museum than in telling his story. After a lack of financial support killed the museum plan, the book regained primacy in his life.

So behold a hybrid: an entertaining American history book
that's also an entertainment book soaked in American history. And
enjoy, as I do, the realization that those whimsical moments in
high school sometime lead you places you never imagined.

Burn, Baby! BURN!

Prologue

Come back with me to Watts, California, in August 1965: the Watts riots.

I'm in bed early. I have to wake up to do my morning soul-music radio show on KGFJ, 1230 on the AM dial. Got to keep burning the way I've been burning since I hit L.A. in February and took over the Negro neighborhoods. I'm falling asleep in my home in Brentwood, fifteen miles and a universe away from the madness, when all of a sudden I hear that chant on the TV news.

"Burn, baby! BURN!"

Wait a minute. That's *mine!* The rioters are screaming it? They can't do that! They can't steal what I invented. They can't twist it around, make it sound like what it's not.

"Burn, baby! BURN!"

This is crazy. I'd been screaming "Burn, baby! Burn! on the radio for two years—'63 in New York and '64 in Chicago. I'd slap a record I loved on the turntable, let it kick in, and shout into the mike: "Burn, baby! Burn! Kids would call up, shouting it back at me. But they weren't talking about rioting. These rioters, they've got it all wrong, and I can feel something terrible in my bones: everybody else is gonna get it all wrong too.

The next day I see TV pictures of the destruction that will eventually take three dozen lives and turn Watts into a moonscape forever captioned with my signature.

I don't know it yet, but "Burn, baby! Burn!" is going to become institutionalized as a radical chant and a political rant—not a tribute to a piece of music that moves your soul. All of a sudden I'm going to be painted not simply as an exciter but as an inciter! An agitator. Now don't get me wrong. Everywhere I'd gone in the sixties and before, I'd been the hottest voice on Negro radio, and nowhere was I hotter than L.A. in '65. I owned that place precisely because I *did* burn. I *did* incite. Hell, yes! I incited my listeners to put their hands on the radio and touch my heart. I incited 'em by holding a fire-and-brimstone church service in which I was the Lord, R&B music was the Old Testament, and the kids were the disciples. You could hear it when they called in on the "Burn, baby! Burn!" line every morning before school: that urgency in their voices, that pride of being part of something so strong.

I'd been working toward this for nearly twenty years, toward that fusion with the audience. Hustled my ass off from nowhere to achieve it. Invented a pack of audacious on-the-air routines that made your jaw drop. Hell, I wanted a riot! But I wanted a riot on the airwaves. I wanted my listeners' hearts to burn, not their homes.

And now some of those very listeners are burning out on the street, and L.A. authorities are asking me to stop shouting my slogan. And I'm trying to figure out how to explain to men like the mayor of L.A., Sam Yorty—old white men—what "Burn, baby! Burn!" means. And I can't find the words, because "Burn, baby! Burn!" is too big for words. It's the essence of everything I've done, learned, believed, preached, absorbed. All the records I've heard, played, produced, promoted. All the history books and artifacts I've collected. All the singers I've bullshitted with. All the times I've wanted to rear back and hurl my soul through the radio at my listeners. All the triumph, all the hurt—rising above all that, celebrating a moment of pure musical perfection that you can't describe but must simply bow to—that's what I mean when I yell "Burn, baby! Burn!" How can I explain to these men where "Burn, baby! Burn!" comes from?

I couldn't back then. I would've had to explain my life to those men, and there was simply no way back then for a black man to explain the duality of a life like mine, a life with one foot in the world of rhythm and blues and the other in the world of collecting black history—two worlds equally alien and unbelievable to those men, who wanted to shut me up.

But I can explain it now.

I must.

I have finally, at seventy-five, found the words.

I recognize at long last, after a quarter-century on the air and forty years of collecting African American historical memorabilia, that something unique and wondrous happened in my life.

You see, I chased history. And all the while, history was chasing me.

I touched and was touched by almost every social and musical and historical current of the last half-century. And all the while I was too busy to notice. Too busy hustling, surviving, supporting my family.

"Burn, baby! Burn!" was just a piece of it.

I've chased down more than six thousand books, paintings, films, toys, pamphlets, letters, and slave documents, all of it to tell the story of three hundred years of the African American experience. Armed with less than a high school diploma, I've chased history into rare-book shops, manuscript dealers' showrooms, antique stores, and rummage sales. Chased it across the ocean to Europe. History has tormented me and terrified me and humbled me and left me trembling with joy—yet I never realized I was a part of it. But now I understand.

I understand that my life is the story of "soul," the most powerful emotional force in the history of American music, the truest representation of black artistry. Soul music is the bonding of gospel music and rhythm and blues, the sacred and the profane. But soul music is more than music—it's about history, how history shapes a race and how that history trickles down to the way we express ourselves. And that's why I feel as compelled to explain the majesty of the Black Eagle (stay tuned) as to rhapsodize about Sam Cooke.

The name is Montague: *MONT-a-gyew.* It's my last name, the only name I use. When I was on the radio, when I was spreading the music of James Brown, Otis Redding, the Temptations, Aretha Franklin, and Wilson Pickett, listeners knew me as Magnificent Montague. Even today, more than thirty years later, it's not uncommon for them to recognize me. They'll hear my voice, or maybe spot my name on a piece of mail, and suddenly I'll be hearing their reminiscences about being sixteen and listening to my show on a tiny transistor radio on a school bus. And inevitably the question will be asked: Why aren't you back on the *radio,* Magnificent? Lord knows they need you to bring some fire to the air.

And I'll shake my head and smile. For my time on the radio was indeed a time of fire. It was a time when music and society and race and technology all exploded like a bomb, a time when black deejays made R&B erupt from that old marketing niche of "race music" and changed the way young Americans—white as well as black—saw their world. To live in that vortex was to touch America's soul and be touched by it.

I started on the air in 1949, and the hottest year of all was 1965, that year Watts burned, the year Pickett sang about meeting his sweetheart in the "midnight hour," the year Otis demanded "respect." I had arrived at KGFJ, a black-oriented AM station on Melrose Avenue early that year, bringing with me that harsh cry of delight I often shouted during a record I particularly enjoyed. My fans would call in and yell "Burn, baby! Burn!" back at me, the same way Rush Limbaugh's crowd calls up these days to say "Ditto!" only with *soul*—just a way of signifying that rare, glorious, sanctified moment in which a record or anything else had taken its art to a new level. Out on the playground a young man might make a twisting hang-in-the-air shot, and you'd hear it from the brothers on the sidelines: "*Burn,* baby!"

The phrase infected Los Angeles's Negro lexicon like a virus, and to my horror, when Watts went up in flames that August, when people began setting buildings and cars afire on Imperial Highway and Avalon Boulevard and Main Street, they triumphantly screamed the most evident and analogous and hip thing at hand: "Burn, baby!"

Back then, as the city reeled, I didn't know what to say in response. For the first two days of the riots I kept using "Burn, baby! Burn!" on the air, like I always did. It was my slogan, not the rioters'. Only as the years went by and my hobby of collecting turned into an obsession with black history did it dawn on me that the right rhetorical response to "Burn, baby!" would have been a tired but true cliche.

"Learn, baby."

Learn about the forces that are controlling you. Learn to dominate them. Learn that your people in America have always struggled against oppression and always will. Learn, in ways that will astonish and inspire you, that they have often won despite odds much greater than those you face.

Learn, for example, about that Black Eagle. Come along with me on the chase for him. Feel my adrenaline pump and my goose bumps rise.

There's a manuscript dealer I telephone once in a while. Last time must have been ten years ago. "Anything for me?" I ask. She says, "No, nothing." One morning years back, when I was still living in Los Angeles, I'm doing my daily exercise workout near my apartment—and I see her on the street with another lady.

I call out in mock defeat, "I'm not gonna get anything from you, am I?"

And she answers, "I think I have something for you, but I'm not sure where it is." Her files are like that.

"What is it?" I ask.

"The Black Eagle."

Well, my heart about stopped.

I had been fascinated with the Black Eagle since I first read about him in the sixties. His name was Hubert Fauntleroy Julian, and you can pick your description of him: soldier of fortune, stunt pilot, diplomat, rum runner, bodyguard, foreign correspondent, mercenary. The crown prince of black aviation. He was born in Trinidad in 1897, was raised in America, and ran into the wall of segregation when he tried to become a military pilot in the thirties. Blacks did not fly for this nation until the 332d Fighter Group—the Tuskegee Airmen— was formed in 1942, a year after the attack on Pearl Harbor. So in 1936 Julian volunteered to fly for Haile Selassie's Ethiopian forces, which were under attack by Italy. He became a colonel.

The Black Eagle was a spectacular man. Six feet tall, 200 pounds, striding through life in a derby, cutaway coat, striped trousers, and spats. I had never been able to obtain a shard of the man's life. But now my friend, the dealer, was offering me a piece.

It was a letter that showed me yet another side of the Black Eagle. Dated September 6, 1940, and written on stationery identifying Julian as a captain in the Finnish Air Force, it described how Finland, which had been attacked by Axis forces five months earlier, had asked Julian to broker the purchase of ten air ambulances. Julian had arranged for a Delaware aircraft company to build the planes and for Finnish pilots to fly them back to their homeland. The Black Eagle would pocket 10 percent of the $529,000 cost.

I had known none of this. Now I did. I had never been able to touch the Black Eagle. Now I could. And so I slipped him into an acid-free folder and put him to sleep with the rest of the people whose glory and foibles I pursue.

The story I want to tell you is how a young man who wanted nothing more than to run his mouth on the radio turned into an older man who wanted nothing more than to collect every intriguing scrap of black history he could lay his hands on—and, finally, turned into an even older man who has taken stock of his journey, and his collection, and wishes to pass it on. For years I have struggled to transform my collection—regarded as one of the largest and best privately held collections of African American artifacts in the United States—into a museum. In recent years I have been forced to concede that this will not come to pass. I am now preparing to auction off the collection. So the story I am about to tell is an effort to accomplish, in literature, what my museum might have been.

My transformation from a radio soul shouter to historian was a stumbling-blind, blithe, yet astonishingly rich passage through all the historical forces that would consume me as a collector. Ten years ago I would have laughed at that suggestion, because I lived the kind of life where, if you were to survive, there was no time to look back or inward.

I started collecting in the fifties, rummaging through used-book stores in my free time, and then becoming obsessed in the sixties. Never expected to get interested in black history because I didn't grow up thinking of myself as black. Oh, I was black, but not *black* black. I didn't feel black. I felt like Montague.

The radio business changed that. Going South changed that. Moving to Chicago changed that. Discovering the blues changed that. Being stirred by soul preachers changed that. Hundreds of raw encounters scraped away my naïveté so that, down the road, fans who heard me moan with pained kinship over Ray Charles's "Let's Go Get Stoned" or Otis Redding's "Mister Pitiful" assumed I was a soul brother off the block, blown onto the air from the corner of some mythical ghetto intersection. "Back it up and gimme four more bars!" I'd yell at the end of a record I wanted to promote (either for a kickback or for pure kicks), and then I'd play the last thirty seconds again and moan over it lovingly. If they only knew the truth about where I came from. Decades later, the *New York Times* and the *Los Angeles Times* would write long flattering articles about my history collection, and readers might well assume I was an educated man. If they only knew where I came from.

Because I couldn't make a decent living just working a microphone, over the years I stuck my fingers into every crevice of the music business. I became a songwriter, a publisher of more than

150 singles and albums, and a record producer. I built my own studios wherever I was a deejay and used them to record new talent. Managed artists, booked shows, got to know people, soaked up a lot, and then one day in Chicago I walked into a used-book store and . . . man, I just got the collecting bug. Working in the racially charged environments of the day, driving through so many cities back when highways still let you see local commerce, and being the kind of person who likes to soak up a variety of influences, I spent more and more time looking for materials defining black history. It was like a private affair at first: there wasn't a lot of competition for memorabilia. Negroes were still relatively invisible in America. And as any collector can tell you, you develop an addictive love of pursuit. You see a fragment, and it fits because of a dozen other seemingly isolated fragments that you've bought over the years. You imagine or crave a certain work, and then one day, out of nowhere, you behold it.

Some of what I own I have never seen another copy of. An example is my thick 1895 book recording all written and spoken tributes after the sudden death of Frederick Douglass, America's leading abolitionist—and that scares me more than it delights. If I hadn't found that book, it might well be consigned to oblivion. Think about it: what happens if *Thoughts and Sentiments on the Evil and Wicked Traffic of the Slavery and Commerce of the Human Species,* written in 1787 by Attobah Cugoano, an African taken to England, is never read? What happens if a tiny, elegant pincushion with an engraving of a black man in chains, called *A Colored Man in the City of New York,* made in 1835 by Patrick Henry Reason, a black artist who worked for abolitionists, is never seen? What happens if Frank Sapp's magnificent 1944 painting of the Haitian general Toussaint L'Ouverture astride a horse, symbolizing the ability of black men and women to throw off colonial chains, is never viewed? (Wherever I've lived, that one has always hung on the most prominent wall.)

Conversely, what happens if you allow people to experience these works, and hundreds like them, in the course of a day? I'll tell you. You throw your so-called contemporary role models in the trash can. You proclaim that these are our role models.

The more I collected, and the longer I remained a deejay, the more my professional life bled into my fascination with the black experience. At a time when blacks had almost no power base beyond their churches, black deejays played a mystical, powerful social role. Whites owned the stations and the unions. We deejays labored in electronic sweat shops, sweltering studios with noisy electric fans, one microphone and two turntables, and heavy headphones. Your on-air nickname might be Zing Zang, but if you messed up they'd fire you and put another Zing Zang on the air tomorrow, and it would be as though you never existed. Barely up from slavery.

Yet despite these hardships—in fact, because of them—successful black deejays enjoyed astonishingly strong, direct communication with a mass audience, a feeling of solidarity that was unprecedented in commercial broadcasting. We were de facto mayors and weekday preachers, masters of a private universe. We were the equivalent of movie stars, the sole link between listeners and the music. No way that happens today. You've got stations being routinely sold for tens of millions of dollars, programming their music on the basis of demographic and "psychographic" studies. The deejays are along for the ride. In my day radio was a seat-of-the-pants business. You worked by your gut.

Until recently I had forgotten a lot about those days. I'm a stubborn kind of fellow, short and wiry and steel on the inside. I hate losing, and like I said, I hated introspection. After Watts burned, I reluctantly let "Burn, baby! Burn!" slip out of my repertoire. In the hands of protesters and people who hated protesters, it became and remains to this day a slogan and an epithet but nevermore a heartfelt compliment. A song couldn't "burn" anymore, and I hated that. My fascination for being on the air ebbed. Programming gurus were already institutionalizing the Top-40 format, playlists were replacing the instincts of the jocks, FM was replacing AM. I went off and built my own station in Palm Springs, right down to driving my own construction equipment.

Gradually, though, I started to think about what had happened to me, where my life fit. I began to recognize that the black experience wasn't merely something that I'd collected. It was something that I'd lived, something that I'd helped shape. If history was chasing me, maybe I'd let it catch up.

I started thinking about sharing my collection so that stories like mine, and bigger than mine, could be told—hundreds of them, thousands of them. I started thinking about taking my collection out of storage in a warehouse and laying it out in a place where history could leap out at you. Where you could walk the path of my people. Where you could not only hear and read about the pain and the glory but feel it. Where the video screens would roll the images and the speakers would burst forth, and the greats, the Booker T. Washingtons and the Frederick Douglasses, would share the podium with the anonymous strugglers.

I wanted you to hold in your hand the 12 ½-cent pamphlet written in 1850 by the fugitive slave Henry Watson. I wanted you to watch silent movies made in 1916 by the black-owned Lincoln Motion Picture Company of Los Angeles. I wanted you to sing along to "It Pays to Serve Jesus," by the Pace Jubilee Singers. I wanted to overwhelm you with the power of the contralto Marian Anderson's Negro spirituals and classics. I wanted to bombard you with computerized special effects to make you well up with tears at the sheer brilliance of Dr. George Washington Carver.

We have the technological power now to show the course of a man's life in the span of five minutes: a sickly Alabama slave child, stolen from his mother, repurchased by his owner for the price of a horse, miraculously rising to earn a master's degree in agriculture, inventing the economic miracle of crop rotation by alternating cotton with peanuts, and then developing more than 100 peanut by-products. Behold a replica of Dr. Carver's laboratory, his letters, an original painting he did with peanut oils. Behold this inspiration—inspiration for all Americans.

I wanted that feeling inside my museum. I wanted, also, to tell these stories to reach the youngsters who have the energy and the intensity to succeed but don't know their history. I wanted to show it to them. These gang members, these hip-hoppers—once they understood their history, there'd be no holding them back. I wanted to give them something more powerful than guns or turntables. I wanted to give them their B.H.D.s, their black history degrees. I wanted to show them how to soar, like the Black Eagle.

But we know not all dreams come true. I know I will not get there. And so I've written the story of how it all came together— the collecting, the music, the wild ride through history in pursuit of history. I used to tell my listeners to put their hands on the radio so I could touch their hearts. Let's do it again: put your hand on this page and turn it, and touch my heart. I don't think you'll be able to stop.

1 The Hustle

I was born on January 11, 1928, in a segregated state—New Jersey. It was a subtle, quiet kind of apartheid. No one in my family ever talked about it. There were no civil-rights fighters among my relatives or the people I knew in my neighborhood. I didn't really know what a white racist was. I saw the black preacher and the black barber, but not the black teacher; mine were white. I knew I was "colored" when I attended the movies, where I had to sit on a certain side of the theater. We could go down to Atlantic City to the beach, on the colored side. (If you were a Negro, you couldn't go to either side after 6 P.M. unless you had a waiter's white jacket.)

I was named Nathaniel Montague, but my first name seemed to slip away soon after my diapers did. People called my father by his last name, and everyone, including my friends, did the same with me. ("You can call him Montague or

Magnificent," my bride would warn her Louisiana family years later. "Take your choice.") My parents, my sister, and I lived in a small two-bedroom apartment in Elizabeth, in northern New Jersey. Our family, like most of the coloreds, had a line of credit at the Jewish market. I didn't venture across to where the few colored doctors or lawyers or schoolteachers lived. They were dressed up in hold-back-the-black attitudes: stay away from me.

In school I didn't feel prejudice outright. My school chums were Italian, or colored, or Jews. At seven or eight my chums and I would laugh and talk on the way home from school and then go our separate ways, but that wasn't commented upon by my family. My mother and father never sat me down and said, "You're colored, you're black, let me tell you how to handle it." I never had my Italian or Jewish friends, or their parents, approach me like that. But I did hear the word *nigger*—of course, I also heard the words *wop* and *kike*. I knew those were the three words to make somebody angry.

I would go to the theater to be entertained. I would laugh and talk on my side of the theater. I loved cowboys. I didn't stop to ask if there was a black cowboy; I didn't know until much later, after I began collecting, that black cowboys had played a part in building the West. I didn't have a clue there were all-Negro movies, either, or know about the courage of the people who founded them, people whose works I would someday acquire. I only knew what Hollywood showed me.

I wasn't religious. Rest of my family was. They'd drag me to the little Church of God—a clapping, singing, crying, Holiness church—but I always sat in "sinner's corner," in the back of the small church. The first few rows in the front, hard up against the choir, were reserved for people who'd been saved. The hand-clappin' aisles. I'm talking about day-and-night church, morning service, afternoon service, young people's group, all this for maybe fifty, sixty members. Holy Rollers (my mother never liked to use that term) are stronger than Baptists. When you put us together we do the same thing; the difference is the Holy Roller in that little church will straight shout out, while the Baptist in the big church will shout out only after he checks to see who's looking.

I didn't want nothing to do with any of it . . . but I didn't want to get my head knocked off, so I went. Now and then my mother would call me up front with the rest, and that preacher would be up there preaching and preaching: "The doors of the church are open. Come up and get saved!" I'd ease on down in my chair in the back; I don't wanna go up there, man. And my mother would look back at me and shake her fist, and that meant one thing: come on up. You go up there. You get on your knees. And they'd be singing, and the guilt'd be on you, that soul singing, that crying. One time, I must have been real young, I went up there, down on my knees, and I just couldn't take any more: I fell asleep. My sister woke me with a nudge, and I leaped up. That was all it took. "He's saved!" the preacher exclaimed. My mother was beaming. The lamb had come in. You were either saved or a sinner in this church, and in my family I was the only sinner. We get home, and I'm arguing with my sister; my mother looks at me and says, anguished, "*You* ain't saved!"

"Well, you *said* I was saved!"

"Boy, what am I gonna do with you?"

Every day my father would give me a Bible verse, and I'd have to try to remember it later in the day. I didn't realize it, but this was my training. I was saved, but in a different way. I was anointed to save souls . . . on the radio. My sister would become an evangelist. I remained secular and soulful.

I loved dramatics, all right, and I was a dreamer, and what I saw in the movies got caught up in my mind, and I wanted to see Hollywood. So in 1941, when I was about fourteen, short and slender and desperate for adventure, I ran away from home. I had no idea how to get to Hollywood. I had no money. I remember hitchhiking, and I was lucky enough to get a moving van headed away from the East Coast. The driver was friendly, said he needed the company, and a couple weeks later I was standing on the corner of Hollywood and Vine.

Now don't get any ideas. I didn't hate my parents; you don't have to have a misunderstanding to leave. I was always different. There was something about that magical movie screen that impressed me. You are your mother's son biologically, but she can't transfer her heart to you. We are not cloned. My parents did instill in me what would make me Magnificent Montague: the gift of gab and the intelligence to interpret events around me, feel their meaning, identify a message. But this was lost on me as a teenager and for a long time afterward. I was wasting my gift, running my mouth, lucky not to get my head bashed in.

I had nowhere to stay when I got to Hollywood. I ended up on Hollywood Boulevard, where I met a guy named Alan Gordon, who happened to be an agent to Ray Milland and Linda Darnell. Because shyness was never my problem, I asked him for a job cleaning up his office, and he said okay. I said, "I ain't got nowhere to stay." He had a bedroom in his office, and he let me stay there.

Nearby were two ritzy nightclubs on the Sunset Strip, the Mocambo and the Trocadero, where it cost you all of two bucks for veal chops. At night I'd go up there and try to make a little money. I'd make a deal with the Mocambo's maître d' and doorman to let me go through the trash; I'd collect newspapers and tin foil from cigarette papers, peel it up, pack it up and sell it to the ragman. The doorman was black but light skinned, from New Orleans, and took a liking to me. He and his family lived next door to "Rochester," the actor Eddie Anderson, in what was called Sugar Hill, off San Vicente Boulevard. The doorman's name was Weaver; his daughter was the cigarette girl at the club. He wouldn't let me stay in his house, but he fixed up a place in the garage for me, and I alternated between living there and at Alan Gordon's office for two or three months.

I knew how to hustle. I'd been one of those little numbers runners in New Jersey, making a dollar picking up slips and money and delivering them to the banker. (Fact was, a dapper black man named Casper Holstein, a West Indian immigrant, invented the numbers game and made a fortune in Harlem in the twenties. The preachers got into it. Sunday morning you'd hear the preacher read from the Bible to the congregation: chapter 3, verse 1 and verse 9, and the Lord said so and so, and tomorrow you gonna see a change—that was his way of suggesting a lucky number to his hungry practitioners. "Now when you leave here today, I want you to remember this verse and this chapter, and tomorrow do accordingly; you gonna have a good day tomorrow." The numbers players loved it, and if they hit, they gave half to the church. Much later I'd collect some of Holstein's correspondence and wonder why no one knew about this man. If Dillinger could capture the nation's imagination, why not Holstein?)

I didn't know it, but Alan Gordon was close to the police, and one day they started talking to me, and they found out I was a runaway. That did it. They sent me up to Ventura, the next county to the north, to a work camp for juvenile runaways awaiting transportation back home. I stayed about a month, until my parents sent the money. I remember a guy with a badge putting me on a train.

My parents had been counting on something more than a street kid. They'd made a huge investment in the future by coming to New Jersey as part of the remarkable exodus of blacks who left the South from the twenties to the forties, one of the periodic waves of Negro migration that resembled the way Jews poured out of Russia in response to the ebb-and-flow of anti-Semitism. "Ain't it hard," went the saying in my people's past, "ain't it hard to be a nigger, for you can't get yo' money when it's due. If you work all the week and work all the time, white man sho' to bring a colored man out behind. Ain't it hard, ain't it hard to be a nigger." The only thing the Negro had left was his wit and laugher. Negroes had flooded out of the South earlier, during Reconstruction, and would again after each of the world wars, bringing to Chicago and Los Angeles the very radio fan base—the electric, family-like, bloodlike connection—that I would tap into.

My parents were both children of former slaves, born around the turn of the century in North Carolina. After marrying they headed to Jersey to escape poll taxes and literacy tests for voter registration. Their only solace was that the past had been even more brutal. That first great westward migration of Negroes during Reconstruction was a mass escape from killing and intimidation during an era when hanging blacks was considered a holiday. Thousands upon thousands of poor black farmers organized committees, contributed their savings, and hired agents to arrange transportation to places like Kansas and Nebraska. One day I'd find a haunting description in a book and understand what these lives had been like: "We wear the mask," wrote Paul Laurence Dunbar, "that grins and lies. / It hides our cheeks and shades our eyes. / This debt we pay to human guile, with torn and bleeding hearts we smile / and mouth with myriad subtleties." My grandparents and parents wore this mask. The greatest challenge of my generation would be to take off the mask and express our true selves to the white world. We would pay a high price.

I was about ten when the Ku Klux Klan marched through Elizabeth in a leafleting campaign that was taking the group through New Jersey and upstate New York, warning about "the Negro situation": "The Negro must be brought again to understand he is a member of an inferior race. . . . the man who does not believe in the supremacy of the white man should get out of America." The KKK understood the significance of our move out of the South, our aspirations, the inevitability of integration—and it frightened them. The sheer size of the march north was daunting: between 1910 and 1920 Alabama lost one-tenth of its black population to migration. Special trains were taking away virtually all the young black adults in small southern towns, and those ol' crackers were crying over the fact no one was left to get in those crops but some old worn-out blacks.

My father, who'd been hired as a manual laborer in the chemical department of DuPont and then laid off, played the violin as a hobby. He was very good and liked to listen to classical symphonic music on the radio, live concerts from New York. He forced me to listen, too. He put an accordion in my hands, and I took lessons for a while. But the only thing that set me apart from other boys, I think, was my imagination. You know how some kids imagine they can ride a horse? I imagined I could travel. And that was why, a few months after I was shipped back to Elizabeth . . .

I up and ran away again.

This time I ended up living in downtown Los Angeles, maybe a less romantic place to you but not to me. I had me a little job, working for an ice company located a block from Pershing Square. Nowadays Pershing is a drug market, but back then I would go there every day to watch the public speakers. It was sort of like London's Speaker's Corner in Hyde Park, where any damn fool can get up and say his piece. That's where all the nuts were. But it got old, and pretty soon I hitchhiked back to New Jersey, and this time my parents sent me to military school, a colored ROTC school, where I stayed less than a year.

While I was in military school, World War II broke out. If you aren't of my generation, you cannot imagine the sense of adventure, possibilities, danger, suspense—it was as if the entire world were up for grabs, especially in those first years of the war, when we not only weren't winning but were encountering some awful times. So by the time I'm sixteen, I'm hanging out with my boyhood chum Tony Williams, and we're talking about what we're gonna do, and Tony says, out of the blue, "I'm gonna join the Merchant Marine."

He could have just as easily said he was going to join the Flying Tigers and I would have gone along.

Tony and I had sung on the street for nickels and dimes, and he'd protected me; if I thought I was going to get into a fight, I'd go get Tony. Tony's mother was religious, and my mother was religious, except my mother was Holiness and his mother was a disciple of Father Divine. I got my mother to sign the enlistment papers, and Tony and I went off to Sheepshead Bay on Long Island to learn how to be merchant seamen. It was like going to boot camp. Within a decade Tony and I would both reach places in show business we couldn't dream about, but for now nothing could surpass the excitement we felt. Didn't matter that I couldn't swim or had never been on the water.

I got my ass kicked in that boot camp. To this day I'll never forgive Tony. I didn't want to be no sailor. I just wanted to jump on those ships and go to the places I'd dreamed about. Thirteen weeks later we got our papers.

When you graduate they assign you to your first ship. During the war they were called liberty ships—private ships that were doing government work, hauling supplies and troops. The government had commissioned 2,700 of them, 14 named after prominent Negroes, including the *Paul Laurence Dunbar,* the *Harriet Tubman,* the *Bert Williams* (after the famed comedian), and the *James Weldon Johnson* (after the noted diplomat and composer of "Lift Every Voice and Sing," the Negro national anthem). Again, I couldn't have cared less—hell, I barely recognized there was a war on. It was early '44 and there we were, two hometown boys headed for danger, not a clue what we'd let ourselves in for.

More than 24,000 Negroes would be employed in the Merchant Marine, working in every capacity aboard ship from radio operator to pharmacist to chief steward. But none of the rest compared to Hugh Mulzac. In 1918 Mulzac became the first Negro in the United States to earn a shipmaster's license and the right to command a merchant ship. It took a while for him to claim that right: for the next twenty-four years he took jobs at sea either as a cook or a steward. Only after the war began, only when the government needed men so badly that it had to drop its blindness, only after pressure by the progressive maritime union, did America give Mulzac command of his own liberty ship: the *Booker T. Washington,* launched in September 1942. Could a teenager imagine, upon shaking Mulzac's hand while waiting at the union hall for a ship assignment, that one day he would have in his possession the correspondence of both Mulzac *and* Washington? Never. I didn't even know who Booker T. Washington was. I only knew I had signed on to life at sea for great pay: $200 a month. I was full of pride; I'd been trained in an integrated setting, the tide of battle overseas was turning, and the North Atlantic awaited me. In the year to come I would cross the Atlantic a dozen times and the Pacific five times.

On board the soldiers we were transporting—black and white, segregated in different parts of what was called a "checkerboard" ship—adopted me as kind of a mascot. Everybody loved me. I started to put on shows. I would find blacks who could sing or dance—so many of them had talent—and then we'd clear a space and put on a show. I'd charge admission—two packs of cigarettes, because they were cheap. I'd take all those cigarettes, and when we got to France, I'd sell 'em. I was also in charge of "hittin' 'em against the wall"—the dice games. I didn't get no money from the dice, but I supplied the refreshments, making sure the cook baked up an extra cake or a pie. Yes, those dice games were segregated, but the food wasn't—I passed back and forth, making a profit on both sides and splitting it with the captain.

Eventually I became a chief steward, in charge of all the food. I talked my way into that. I learned how to cook, but not that well, so I would sign on with the maritime union for an assignment as the second cook and baker and pay the chief cook to do my share; it was better than having to be a mess boy. Then next trip, or another ship, I'd become chief steward and pay the second cook half my salary to help me with the menu preparation. The way the union worked, the longer you'd been on the beach—without a ship—the better standing you had to bid on a particular job.

But there was no one I could pay off to spare me the hell of the North Atlantic. I spent many nights on watch for German subs; those wolfpacks were always on the prowl, looking to knock off our undermanned ships. We only had a five-man navy gun crew with a thirty-five-millimeter gun to help us. The rest of us were trained to man the defenses if the sailors were knocked off. Our only security lay in never leaving the convoy that was protected by navy battleships, but when your ship broke down, you had to navigate to the nearest port without an escort. I saw men go overboard we couldn't rescue—the waves were that strong. And when the bow of the ship would finally come up, there'd be a German sub looking you dead in the face, and they would pick you off any way they wanted—there might be one hundred liberty ships and only ten escorts spread across the sea. Many times we were alone, and many times I was no longer excited but scared to death. What I feared most, like all the men, was being in the water after a torpedo hit. We knew you would get numb and freeze before help arrived. It made a man of me quick. I slept with my life preserver and my clothes on, and we took those life preservers into the shower with us. I was so determined never to be without my life preserver that I took a bath only when I couldn't stand the stink; I wasn't going to get in that water naked.

I saw the raw side of segregation up close for the first time. On the ship black soldiers associated primarily with each other, and the USOs in England and France were segregated. I wasn't mad at anybody about it. I was busy enjoying life. In France the people seemed to like the black soldiers, and they really liked me because I was selling chocolates I'd been storing. Once, in Le Havre, some Frenchmen came aboard and asked to see the black captain; since I'd been selling, that's who they presumed I was. It was a day we were supposed to up anchor and sail at 16:00; well, a few hours before, everybody was saying the ship was drifting. They finally figured out why: there was no anchor. I'd sold it to those Frenchmen—they wanted to buy the anchor chain, and the only way to get it was to pull up the anchor . . . and without the chain, there was no way to use the anchor. The real captain had to buy the anchor back. Like I said, I was young! Everybody was selling everything! I wasn't thinking about the consequences.

Segregation accomplished one thing: it created a bond between Negroes. The war was really when the homeboy relationship got started, when you had to rely on your brothers no matter who they were. It was so bad in England that white MPs were arresting Negro soldiers and seamen for dancing with white girls, asking for IDs, locking them up. There were many fights. The English women loved the black soldiers, and the Southern white soldiers couldn't stand to see a jigaboo with a white lady. When I first got to England, they asked me where my tail was—honest. The white soldiers had been spreading rumors that black soldiers had tails.

But you see, a man has to have a context for this to really sting, and I wouldn't develop mine for a long time. I remember being in Belfast and feeling loved. The people would come up and want to touch my hair; I was a celebrity just for being a Negro! They brought me into their homes. It didn't matter that I didn't understand half the words they were saying. I sold 'em some chocolates, sold 'em some cigs. They'd give me their addresses to write them when I got back. The British people, they loved the Negroes. The only problem we had was with our fellow white Americans. Funny, though: at the same time, wherever you could hear Negro jazz and blues was where you found a handful of hip whites, that small cadre of rebels. Every black military outfit had music. White soldiers would come into our hotspots, take a corner, segregate themselves, and dance until the white MPs put them out. (That's right, only white MPs could arrest whites.) How could I have imagined that twenty years later, some of these white soldiers' children, rebelling in their own way, would penetrate radio's still-segregated walls, find me on the dial, and secretly adopt me?

After one of my last trips, Tony and I were back in New York, and he told me he was leaving, didn't want to sail any more. We went up in Harlem and cut "Danny Boy," just for fun, in a little recording booth in a five-and-dime store. By the time I saw Tony again, he would be recording in elaborate circumstances.

I must have sailed everywhere: to Holland; to Russia, a "suicide run" that paid extra money; to Normandy, two months after the huge invasion. We brought thousands of members of the fabled Redball Express, the Negro port battalions that "redballed" it through France on old muddy roads (or new ones that they built), bringing in the heavy equipment that allowed the front-line troops to penetrate Hitler's hold on France. Their theme song was an old Negro spiritual. It was so difficult on those roads they'd sing "Keep-a Inchin' Along"—that's how they moved sometimes, inch by inch, night and day, moving food and ammo, you name it, driving twenty-two out of twenty-four hours, sometimes dying falling asleep. One trip over, we brought the 761st Negro Battalion, which

tore through France, Austria, and Germany for 183 days, demol-
ished three towns, and caused 128,000 German casualties. "Everyone has their eyes on you—don't let me down," General Patton
told them. And they didn't. (But when that Patton movie came
out, there wasn't a black speck on the horizon; white like snow.)
When we dropped the 761st off at the French port, those men
loaded me up with mail. "Monty," they called me. That night at the
colored club, a jazz band played; the French gals loved to dance the
American jive, the lindy, the jitterbug, but all the Negro soldiers,
aware of what they were about to face, were lonesome to be with
their brown-skinned women.

The white soldiers had their pinup queen, Betty Grable. They
would kiss her buns for luck and roll their dice, and they resented
Negro soldiers who dared to pin up Grable over their bunks or kiss
her buns; it was unthinkable to kiss her for luck. But what the white
GIs didn't know was that our own colored GIs had a queen who
became official while we were aboard ship. We called her Miss Fine
Brown Frame, Lena Horne—she could sing and dance, and she had
passion and fire in her eyes and a fine rumble seat fit for a king.

Near the end of the war our liberty ship landed in South Africa.
I was confused by the contradictions I saw. I'd been told in grade
school that Africans were wild, inferior to whites. Before we
landed, the captain called the crew together to tell us what was
required in Cape Town and the other South African cities we'd be
visiting—most specifically, what was required of the Negro sailors.
This was the first time I had heard the word *apartheid*. I was
stunned: how could South Africa, with such a huge majority black
population, be in this position? The captain warned the Negroes
that we could not mix with white South Africans, that police
would not know we were Americans until they heard our accents,
and that we should not get into local discussions about the plight
of Negroes in America. Of course, we all agreed to the rules, but I
had no intention of obeying orders (except for the black-only
signs—they would make us feel at home).

The eight Negroes on board were anxious to touch our motherland and meet the Africans and hear them speaking Bantu and shake their hands—was this not our ancestral home? Since I was the youngest seaman on board and the second cook and baker, I came into contact with the African dockworkers and struck up a good relationship. We had to feed them when they worked aboard ship. I could hardly understand their English, but at night I got invited to their hut in the countryside to see them dance. Their rhythm put American Negro rhythm to shame. They danced for love, for grief, for hate, for prosperity, to pass the time. Every night I was caught up in African emotion, rhythmical movement, and the most alluring costumes, their pantomimes performed to music. They looked at me strange; I looked the same way back, but I was in awe.

I got a chance to learn about the drum, the basis of African music, its variety almost unlimited. I watched and listened to blacks talking and answering, the tiny timbo drum hung around their necks. I saw and heard every possible combination of sound that could be produced by striking a tight skin, a piece of wood, or metal with the hand, the way the pitch or tone could be changed. I could not possibly understand the talking drum, which imitates speech, but I believed in it.

I began to feel immense pride of race and culture. I went to a Zulu gathering. Man, I was scared to death. They had the white paint, they did a dance called the dead cannibal dance, the hunting dance. When they do that, people just go into a frenzy. It had the same effect as if I was in my mother's Holiness church, when they would shout and sing and talk in tongues.

I went to Liberia. I thought I was in America! During abolition times missionaries had helped ex-slaves and freedmen settle there. Saw Nigeria for a day. Man, I was in heaven. Met these statuesque, sophisticated people, blue-black. The few Negroes with me, they were just as fascinated. Then to the Mediterranean, through the Rock of Gibraltar, through Alexandria, Egypt—*they* were colored!— Senegal, the Persian Gulf, back to England, and then back home.

"Monty," the Negro troops would say to me ruefully as my ship

headed back to the United States, "you gonna have all them girls
for yourself. Kiss 'em when you get home for us." What they didn't
know was that I was shy and still a virgin. I got home about the time
the war got over, but I wasn't through sailing, and I sure wasn't
through exploring.

2 The Groove

Growing up I was a radio junkie. I
loved the voices I heard, the great
radio voices of people like Gabriel
Heatter, the newsman, and Martin
Block, the pioneer disc jockey. I
loved the sense of carrying myself
like a performer. If you live long
enough, you figure out what you
were destined for, why things happen. Was it an accident, for example, that my father slapped an
accordion in my hands and sent me
to an Italian teacher? Why, though I
soon put the instrument away out
of uninterest, did I rediscover it
forty-five years later—and still have
one in my home? Why were Tony
Williams and I performing in the
street—him singing, me dancing—
as little kids? What led me, on those
troop ships, to stage shows, to have
a guy playing sax and keep him behind a curtain, silhouetted, picking
a dramatic moment for him to step
out? Where does the theatricality
come from? I don't know where I

got the bug for radio, but anyone who lived through President Roosevelt's fireside chats during the thirties, when I was just beginning to notice the world, would understand. Imagine the raw intensity in every living room as a desperate nation focused on that box, that voice. Tell me what kind of communal experience today compares to that? The Super Bowl? That's once a year. We had it every time Roosevelt opened his mouth.

After the war ended, I kept sailing with the Merchant Marine as it returned to its civilian mission of hauling goods all over the world. It was a great gig: whenever you wanted to travel, or ran out of money, you'd go down to the union office and bid on a job—a trip—and there was plenty of work. For somebody who was now all of eighteen, with no restrictions on his life, who'd already seen the world at its worst, it was a magical key, and for years I kept turning it: traveling, coming home to Jersey for a while, and traveling again.

It was on one of those times home in 1947—between sailing jobs, looking for something to keep me off the streets—that a cousin of mine named Ramond Bruce got me a job. Ramond had become the first Negro disc jockey in Philly earlier in the forties. I'd bring food off the ships to him, and sit there and listen to him do his show, and that's where I got the bug to get on the mike. I never was on the air, but he let me go out and sell his accounts—his sponsors—and carry his record box. I was like his ass kisser, his amen corner. I learned how to sell, and I learned something about R&B music. (This was actually a couple years before anybody used the term *rhythm and blues;* it was still called "race" music, and you could see that term on the labels of the records that came to Ramond from the record companies.) It was an awakening for a boy who mostly dug jazz. And then, back to sea I went: Nagoya, Japan; Panama and the canal; Brisbane, Australia.

Sometime in 1949 we docked for a while in Boston, and I got another job selling radio time, on WVOM in Brookline, Mass. I was pissed off at Ramond because he wouldn't let me on the air with him. What I'd learned was that the marketplace—not just the talent of your tongue—was what made you a deejay: if you could sell time to a sponsor, you could host a proportionate amount of radio time—figure fifteen minutes for each client you brought in, for starters. Selling came natural, talking came natural, and so there I was, sitting in a Jewish-owned record shop on Tremont Street in Boston, calling myself "Jumping Jack Montague," doing a show fifteen minutes at a crack, starting off with a live interview with Frankie Laine, not knowing what the hell questions to ask, knowing almost nothing about him, grateful for his willingness to coach me off the air.

It was straight hustle. I wasn't a paid staff announcer, wasn't making anything from being on the air beyond a cut of the advertising I could sell. If I wanted more airtime and money, I had to find more sponsors. The Negro market was wide open; it was just a matter of canvassing those little businesses that catered to blacks—liquor stores and beauty supply places (little by little you could break off lots of chunks of this huge economy, which was unknown to white institutions like radio)—and selling them small blocks of time. Frankie Laine had been kind enough to suggest to WVOM's management that, since they now had a Negro on the air, it might make sense to book some black acts and let me interview them. It turned into a little call-in show and made me the first Negro radio personality in New England.

I knew a guy who booked jazz dances, and from time to time I'd announce for him, down at Revere Beach, when they'd allow the blacks to go down. This promoter would have an evening for blacks and an evening for whites. There were no so-called black-oriented shows on the radio, so to promote the jazz dances I'd get a loudspeaker and drive around with it in a car, like you'd try to build heat for a political rally. Eventually somebody at WVOM thought about putting the dance on the radio station to reach the white kids. The station hired a big-time announcer to cut a spot, but the guy who owned the jazz dance club didn't like the way it came out, and he asked me to do it. The station ran the ad, and it worked. And so, come Saturday night, there I was, doing a remote broadcast from the club, spinning records—R&B, blues like Memphis Slim's "Messin' Around," jazz from Erroll Garner—and emcee-ing the show. Was I prepared? Not on your life. I winged it, just like I'd winged Frankie Laine's interview. My gift, talking as fast as I could think, saved me. "Roll up the rug, push back the chair! Jumpin' Jack Montague is on the air!" I shouted. That was my first slogan.

I was indebted to the club owner, who was Jewish. It was the first in a profoundly long list of times when a Jewish person extended himself to me. People don't want to give other people credit, but hear me: I love the Jews. Without them, I would be an ignorant SOB right now. We are plagued, at times, by some pitiful anti-Semitic talk by a few black "leaders," but the truth is that black folk know in their hearts, just like Jewish folk know in theirs, the indelible historical bond we share. Many times Negro slaves sang songs within their master's earshot of that great day when they would flee "Egypt"—a transparent metaphor for getting the hell out of the South.

Funny, then, that one of the most notorious anti-Semites of my race was coming up in the Boston area at the same time I was on the air there, and our musical paths crossed. He was a charismatic West Indian calypso singer named Louis Eugene Wolcott who called himself Calypso Gene, going for that Harry Belafonte sound. He grew up black in a predominantly Jewish neighborhood and was a couple years younger than me. Fooling around in a studio once, I produced a recording of his singing that I hear collectors with a political bent are dying to get their hands on.

But Calypso Gene wasn't going to stay in the music business long. The bitterness he brought with him from his childhood exploded a few years later, at age twenty-five, when he went to a rally given by Elijah Muhammad's Nation of Islam and was, seemingly, reborn as devoted follower of Elijah. Calypso Gene became first Louis X (in Black Muslim tradition, the "X" symbolizes how the true heritage of African Americans was stolen during the slave trade) and then, as he remains today, Louis Farrakhan.

A long time later I would become a friend of Malcolm X—the

more famous Nation of Islam spokesman who eclipsed Farrakhan within the hierarchy of the Black Muslims and was assassinated because of factional differences. I felt no brotherhood with Elijah Muhammad or the doctrine of racial separatism. But I do understand what Calypso Gene must have gone through, that moment of racial awakening he experienced in 1955 when he saw Elijah Muhammad speak, an awakening that prodded him within a few years to record distinctly un-Belafonte songs like "The White Man's Heaven Is the Black Man's Hell." Because at age twenty-four I experienced precisely the same kind of awakening at the feet of a man equally inspiring and—I believe history will document—so much greater.

His name was Paul Robeson.

I had left my infant deejay career after a year or so to get back to sea as a merchant sailor, back to adventure. I wasn't walking away from all that much. After several trips, including a stunning one to South America, where I first saw the tall, majestic, bronzed cocoa- and black-skinned Brazilians, I returned to New Jersey for some time ashore. It was late 1951, and there I was, up in Harlem, 125th Street and 7th Avenue, face to face and shaking hands with a giant of a man, looking up into his deep, passionate eyes, intelligent forehead, and listening to his voice, deep as the roar of a lion, yet smooth and melodious. My soul was caught up in a peacefulness I had never felt before. It was an outdoor conference for equal rights for Negroes in the arts, sciences, and professions, and Robeson was one of the key speakers—today, in my memory of the event, the only speaker.

Try to imagine hearing this revolutionary voice during a time when segregation was still legal, when the notion of socially compensating the black race for slavery was a joke, a pipe dream, compared to the simple torture of getting through the next day under Jim Crow, a time before *Brown v. Board of Education* or Martin Luther King Jr. or Rosa Parks. And into this mess strides a celebrity who, by his sheer talent, has penetrated the line between black and white, who could have taken his pot of gold and left the struggle yet has chosen to press on the most sensitive nerve in America. Try to imagine you are a Negro who unquestionably accepts your fate the way a cat accepts being put out at night.

Try to imagine, in other words, hearing your first "race man."

"We are here today," Robeson began,

> to work out ways and means of finding jobs for colored actors and colored musicians, to see that the pictures and statues made by colored painters and sculptors are sold, to see that the creations of Negro writers are made available to the vast American public. To see that the way is opened for colored lawyers to advance to judgeships—yes, to the Supreme Court of the United States, if you please. [That last notion was fifteen years away; we all would have bet on fifty or a hundred.]
>
> Yes, we are dealing with a great people. Their very survival testifies to that. One hundred million sacrificed and wasted in the slave ships and on the cotton plantations in order there might be built the basic wealth of this great land. Not only have the Negro people survived in this America, they have given to these United States almost a new language, given it ways of speech, given it perhaps the only indigenous music, one giant creation—modern popular music, whether it be in the theater, film, radio, records—wherever it may be, almost completely based upon the Negro idiom.

This was a dangerous man! Now, if I'd had a shred of political awareness, maybe I wouldn't have been as surprised. I was, after all, part of the maritime union, an aggressive, leftist union, part of the old CIO (the progressive, gutsy part of what became the AFL-CIO later in the decade). People like Robeson were the only reason Hugh Mulzac had ever become a ship's captain during the war—straight-out progressive pressure. I might as well have still been sixteen, for all I'd learned, staring, open-mouthed, at what I was hearing.

"There is no leading American singer, performer of popular song, whether it is a Crosby, a Sinatra, a Shaw, a Judy Garland, who had not listened and learned by the hour to Holiday, Waters, Florence Mills, Bert Williams, to Fitzgerald, and to the greatest of all, Bessie Smith. Without these models, who would have heard of a Tucker, a Jolson, a Cantor?"

"Go into the field of dance," he thundered as though God were speaking through him. "Where could there have come an Eleanor Powell without a Bill Robinson? How could Artie Shaw and Benny Goodman have appeared but for a Teddy Wilson, a Hall Johnson [who headed up big spiritual choirs], a Will Marion Cook [the turn-of-the-century composer who built the first musical show out of our lively syncopated rhythms, popularizing ragtime]?"

This was a man who spoke twelve languages. The son of an escaped slave, an interpretive artist, a Renaissance man, an All-American football star, a scholar, an orator, a star of theater, film, and concert stage, a patriot who'd led black entertainers like Lena Horne and Louis Armstrong through army camps to entertain Negro soldiers—a man who was at this very moment being persecuted by congressional red-hunters for his principled views on Negro rights, views that would be perfectly mainstream within a decade but at this moment were frighteningly radical and were costing him millions of dollars in potential income, costing him his passport, his ability to share his gifts with the world, embittering him against a country he was willing to love despite all its hypocrisy.

"Whence stems even Gershwin?" he demanded of us. "From the music of Negro America, joined with the ancient Hebrew idiom. Go and listen to some of the great melodies. Here again is a great American composer, deeply rooted, whether he knew it or not, in an African tradition very close to his own heritage. I speak very particularly of this popular form. This is very important to the Negro artists. Because billions, literally billions of dollars have been earned and are being earned from their creation, and the Negro people have received almost nothing."

The Negro people. Had I ever, until this moment, thought about myself seriously as a member of the Negro people? It was all too much to simply stand here and feel this explosive notion flow through my loins: the white world that inexorably dominated

mine was not superior but in fact had gained some of its luster from
my people. The surge I'd felt when I was on the microphone in
Brookline was wrapped up in something more than me; it was connected to the Negro people, to history.

"So we are dealing with the people who come from great
roots—of a proud people, rich in tradition: [W. C.] Handy, one of
the creators of the blues. Count Basie, colored arranger receiving
a pittance while white bands reap harvests. What heartbreak for
every Negro composer. Publishing houses taking his song for nothing and making fortunes."

He was singing a freedom song in every language. He was speaking in a dialect that presaged Malcolm X. He was so far ahead of his
time, too far ahead of his time.

"Let us touch for a moment on radio and television. We all
know the difficulties. No major hours with Negro talent. An occasional guest appearance eagerly awaited by the Negro audience. In
the American Guild of Musical Artists, and in the American Federation of Radio Artists [a union I would be forbidden from join-
ing in years ahead], they are shouting an awful lot these days about
how democratic and American they are. Let them show it."

I know he said these things because his remarks were
prepublished in a flier that was handed out, one that I instinctively
kept and still possess. I was so inspired, and yet I did not understand his words' true meaning. They were too sweeping. I was a
Negro, I was deprived, but I hadn't felt the hand slap of society that
Robeson was talking about. I hadn't tasted the hunger. I was still
blind. And yet I tingled. He'd woken me up. He'd let me know, a
quarter-century into my life, that I was a Negro. That force, that
sense of connectedness, would stay with me my entire life. But it
would not kick in just yet. For the next couple of years my life
would remain a series of adventures for the sake of adventure, back
and forth on merchant ships, living a life often very much apart
from what Negroes in America were experiencing—and, more
importantly, cut off from the aspirations they were beginning to
feel. I was still obsessed with traveling the world, broadcasting here

and there whenever it struck me, like the few weeks in '52 when I got off a Merchant Marine ship in Long Beach, California, and sold time to a furniture store so I could do remotes from the shop over KFOX.

It was not until 1954 that another merchant ship I was on finished its assignment in the strangest, most exotic and frightening place I had ever been, a place that would define my style, my soul, my love, my very essence.

3 The Rhythm

That place was Texas.

What could be more foreign than to step off a ship in Galveston Bay? There'd been no warning signs—no gradual entry via train or motor coach, no incremental tightening of the invisible noose that slid around the neck of a colored man as he headed into these parts. I'd seen Africa, seen Europe, seen all shades, all mindsets—but I'd never been south.

I got off a merchant ship in Galveston in '54 because a seaman friend of mine had told me he owned a record shop there. Somehow I heard about a station in nearby Beaumont that was looking for a jockey, and the bug bit me again.

By now music was a more defined commodity than what I remembered from my short stints on the air: rhythm and blues had solidified behind a handful of labels and performers that were committed to a strong style—none of which, of course, I knew anything about. The young, confident, fast-talking man of twenty-six who arrived in Beaumont at the moment when southern music was about to take over the North, when black music was about to take over the white world, when young people were about to take over the planet—that hip Negro hustler didn't have no soul.

I didn't have *no* soul.

I knew, externally, what race meant. I knew the facts of discrimination. What I didn't know, because I had never been there, was the South, or the forces that shaped the South. That dab of segregation in the military—that had seemed temporary. This felt permanent, heavy, a wall one could not walk around.

I talked my way into a job on KTRM at the top of the dial, between 1450 and 1500. It wasn't just segregated black to white. There was a Ukrainian hour, a Jewish hour, a Polish hour—everything was keyed to the ads you could sell. What they didn't have was a black jockey. They had never had one.

I found out why.

Condition number one of my job was: stay the hell out of the station.

That's right, boy, don't come in. I started to get some soul, all right. I had some hard lessons to learn, and I got beat up a couple of times. I didn't know how to say sir or ma'am. I didn't know how a double society functioned. I didn't know the language of southern blacks. I thought I was hip, but I was northern hip, and the South was languid, ad-libbed. I came down knowing more about jazz than rhythm and blues, so artists like Muddy Waters and Howlin' Wolf and B. B. King and Junior Parker and Bobby Bland and labels like Chess and Checker and Atlantic and Specialty were new to me.

I sold an hour or two a day of advertising time, and instead of playing the music in the studio, I took it outside. I did my show remote. I found a black restaurant that would let me deejay live. They set me up in one of their booths, and from 6 to 8 P.M. I was on. I picked up the tricks. I saw people finger-snapping while they were listening in the club, and I started doing it on the air. Still, it was alien to me. I was an eastern square. I mean, they would call me aside and say, "You ain't gonna make it that way, boy!"

"What do you mean?"

"Well, in the first place, you're talking too proper."

So I struggled to pick it up from them.

What saved me was church.

We had a preacher on the station who did a Sunday show for shut-ins; he called it "The Little Green Church on the Hill." No records, just preaching. Sometimes I'd get asked to fill in, but I wasn't good at it—I didn't have the melody; I didn't have the rhythms. It forced me to concentrate on how that preacher of my mother's church operated, how black preachers generate the power they do. Fire and brimstone scared the hell out of me; for everything I've told you about the yelling in my mother's church, the fact was up north they weren't fire and brimstone. Gradually, listening to this radio preacher, it began to sink in. I began to realize how black southern preachers, although not free, were privileged. They and their fathers were the first true rappers, speaking in rhythm and rhyme, strutting up and down the pulpit, talkin' falsetto, talkin' trash, connecting biblical heroes and sinners and backsliders to contemporary life.

I began to realize how the poor whites and Negroes had the same problems, the same sorrows, and how that made it so easy for southern whites to pick up on our music and for the white southern deejays to begin imitating us, since in some markets Negro announcers were only permitted to be on the air on Sundays. And I began to realize how that, in turn, was creating a pent-up audience of curious white teenagers who wanted to explore a hidden world from the safety of their bedrooms: Willie Mabon singing "Poison Ivy," Little Walter drawling "You're So Fine," Howlin' Wolf exploding on "Forty-Four," Lowell Fulsom pleading on "Reconsider Baby," the Spaniels saying goodnight with a kiss on "Goodnight, Sweetheart, Goodnight"—all the real life and emotion that awaited the kids but had been kept hidden from them so far. I began to realize how all this was tied into the sounds I was hearing from that radio preacher, and when he would miss a Sunday and I'd take his shift, I would mock him: "And the Loooooord said . . ." I began stealing my personalities from a lot of unknown black preachers and artists of the South. I want to be honest about it. Without them, there'd be no Magnificent Montague. They had the timing, the drama. Everybody has it in their heads that black people are born with that, but I didn't know how to *dance,* man. And I certainly didn't know anything about the history of where these styles came from, how deeply they were rooted in work songs that helped slaves survive in the field and adjust to the new land: the Negro spirituals, full of joy, beauty, sorrow; the coon shouts; the call and response. I didn't know that Ma Rainey begot the Dinah Washington records I was playing in Texas. I didn't realize the Africanism in me was getting ready for hundreds of soul shows in the years ahead. Later, as a collector, I would gasp as I began to fill in the mosaic, recognizing how many pieces of culture—how much history—I had swiped and organized without paying attention. Right now I was just scuffling to create a style.

I did it so well I almost got myself killed.

All because of a simple market fact.

Let me pose it to you as a question: who controls the purse strings? Who do you think those advertisers care about most?

Right, women.

So who do you think I focused my show on? Who do you think I read my original romantic poetry to? Who do you think I started to call "my darlings," telling them not to let their men treat them like dogs?

And who do you think showed up one day in white sheets?

Yep, men.

White men.

The "problem" was that the only black jockey on the station was attracting a surprising number of white female listeners and callers. So the manager called me inside and introduced me to the assembled gentlemen of the Ku Klux Klan.

"By God, you been makin' love to white ladies, boy!" one of the crackers complained. Boy this, boy that. Uppity, uppity.

The manager jumped in to save his own scalp: "Montague, didn't I tell you to stop that?"

I knew I was dead—when in walked another jockey, J. P. Richardson, a white man, a respected figure on the air, a man who loved the R&B music I was playing, who would come by the restaurant from time to time and sit next to me while I was broadcasting, who'd talk about how he admired the way I could switch to falsetto, talk in rhythm, go to a higher register. "All Negroes seem to have that touch," he'd marvel. "I try to get it myself. That's why I try to be hep."

J. P. faced down the Klan that day. He told them off. He saved my job and, for all I know, my skin. Some of you know what happened next. All that songwriting J. P. was doing on the side paid off. He cut a big record called "Chantilly Lace" as the Big Bopper and was just beginning to enjoy his fame when he crashed in a plane also carrying Buddy Holly and Ritchie Valens in 1959.

I broke out of Beaumont before '54 was out. I wanted a bigger city: Houston.

The way I see it, every black person alive understands Houston, whether they've been there or not, even if they didn't come from the South: Jim Crow, but filled to the brim with Negro culture. Steamy nightlife. The blues. Bobby Bland. Johnny Ace. Willie Mae Thornton. And a man who made the difference in setting the stage for the future of rhythm and blues, a showman, a promoter, the builder of the first black-owned record-pressing plant, and the owner of the largest booking agencies in the South: Don Robey, the owner of the Duke and Peacock labels.

By now I knew enough about the music to work it. The Negro station was KCOH, a white-owned station, black-oriented, all Negroes on the air, and you had to be qualified . . . and the most important qualification was to know your place. You could be the worst thing on the air, but it was the only station the Negroes had. So as long as you played the records, the owner didn't care how much you mumbled.

I walked into the office calling myself the Great Montague and said I wanted a job. Said I'd been recommended by the Big Bopper. That was a lie; all he'd told me was that the station existed. I told the owner I'd been brokering time in Beaumont.

Nothing open now but weekends, he says. I tell him I need work every day.

Where you from? East. How much experience? "Bouncing around since '49, nothing steady, a stint in the Merchant Marine."

"Merchant Marines? I have an uncle in the Merchant Marines!" This opens the door a crack. He asks me if I can sell time.

"Darn straight I can."

"Well, we've been thinking about putting a colored salesman on. If you get out and sell your own time, we'll give you 15 percent and a $50-a-week salary."

I know I'm not gonna let this last, because I gotta get on the mike. But okay, I take the sales job. The owner gives me one piece of advice: "Lemme tell you something, boy. When you talk to me, put a handle on my name." I was still forgetting my "Misters."

I sold a few spots, and I monitored the station. The jocks were dull. I went by one of the busiest shops in Houston, a white men's clothing store on Main. The owner had bought time on the station but stopped because he didn't get the results he wanted.

"Where you from?" he says. "You sound like you're from back east. I'm from New York and down here running my father-in-law's business."

I noticed his name was Cohen. "I been 'round Jewish people all my life," I volunteered. "You ain't nothing but a converted Negro."

And he laughed!

He told me to come back at closing time. We sat and talked about Coney Island, all those things. "Let me be frank with you," I told him. "I don't know how to handle these crackers. Let's combine: lemme do a fifteen-minute show, you buy it, lemme make a hundred a week out of it, pay seventy-five of that to the station, and I'll make a couple of appearances at the store." In six weeks I was doing three hours of time for him, and sponsors like Orange Tommy and Southern Select beer followed. I put on live shows from Club Matinee and I got hot. Negroes in Houston had never heard anyone spouting poetry like this. The clothing store was spending $600 a week on advertising and making enough money to open a second shop, this one in the black Fifth Ward. The station didn't know it, but I was getting a 5 percent cut of the action.

I started to hear murmurings that I had a white audience, too. Remember when all this is happening: for years now white kids have been able to track down that hard-edged R&B music on black stations, a kind of rebellion you might equate to smoking cigarettes at fifteen. In Memphis a white deejay named Dewey Phillips, who specializes in playing black music, has broken his own reverse color line by playing Elvis Presley's first record—summer of '54.

In the midst of this Don Robey calls me one day and says, "Come on by the studio." He tells me he has a dub to play for me. "Drop some poetry in front of it and see what happens."

The song was called "Pledging My Love," by Johnny Ace, a twenty-five-year-old who'd been a star for the past couple of years. Here was the thing about Don Robey: when he asked you to do something, you did it. You didn't run an independent record company in those days, let alone a black independent record company, without being tough. Robey had run a gambling parlor, a supper club, and a record store in Houston before entering the business in '49, and starting with his recordings of Gatemouth Brown, he'd figured out how to get into the R&B Top 10. Elvis's "Hound Dog" came from Don Robey: In '53 he'd put out Willie Mae Thornton's original, written by those magical white boys Jerry Leiber and Mike Stoller.

Robey was a very light-skinned man—I almost mistook him for a cracker when I met him, till I heard the soul pouring out of his mouth. I think there was some Creole in him. You accepted Don on his terms. Little Richard had tried recording for Peacock when he was a nobody and got beaten up by Robey. Richard is still complaining that Robey hit him so hard in the stomach it gave him a hernia. White record companies were trying everything they could to stop Robey from getting needed airplay; they would get to the underpaid Negro jockeys first, paying them under the table to pack the playlist with the white companies' black artists so there'd be no room for Robey by the time he got his records to market. But Don just smiled. He never had trouble fighting back.

I learned so many of my first lessons at this big robust man's feet. Duke-Peacock was the first real recording studio I entered, the first time I saw a session, the first time I saw records pressed, the first time I saw and learned about marketing and promotion. I was overwhelmed, over my head, but Don Robey saw some raw talent in me. He taught me how to edit my free-verse poetry, bought me my first conga drum, introduced me to the old-time bucket Negro musicians, the patriarchs of the blues—made me hear, with my own ears, the Negro dialect, pure folk stories, Negro spirituals in full tone, homemade guitars, southern hand clapping. He let me see, in music, all my ancestral characteristics.

So when Don asked me to put some poetry in front of a dub, you know I was going to do it. I opened up, in a low, throaty voice, leaving plenty of time between the sentences:

"I'll never let you go," I spoke. "You're all my dreams combined in one; the radiance of my rising sun. That's why I'm pledging my love to you." And I hit the song.

Christmas night '54, I was backstage at a concert in Houston. Johnny Ace was on the bill. His recording "Pledging My Love" had not come out yet. He and a bunch of guys were fooling around with a gun, spinning the barrel. They were goading him, and what happened next was the same old Russian roulette story you've heard a hundred times. Johnny Ace killed himself. Robey put the record out posthumously, and it stayed at number one on the R&B charts for ten weeks.

It was a hell of a way to have your biggest hit, but Don was only getting started. He was the one who gave Bobby Bland his middle name, "Blue," and he signed Junior Parker. But what transfixed me was a gospel group he came up with, the Five Blind Boys, with lead singer Archie Brownlee. I've never heard a black man sing with such soul and back-home gospel spirituality as Archie. I froze along with the other people when I heard the falsetto twisting notes, preaching in slow motion, crying in melody, on fire with the Holy Ghost, uninhibited—my God, how scary, and how tearful my eyes were in the radio studio as the record played. And then he'd stop in the middle of all the verses, interpret one of them like a preacher, bring it on home, smooth. Stop again. And say, "I'm here to save some souls." Don sent the Blind Boys on the road. They played for nearly every Negro congregation in the country, and some white ones. They made 'em shout and dance the holy dance. Whenever the Blind Boys came to town, everyone would say God came with 'em.

After maybe a half-year in Houston I heard about some wide-open country on the gulf—that same place I'd originally landed, Galveston Bay. Somebody told me about KTLW, a little "dollar-a-holler" station (meaning that you could buy an ad for a buck or two) with a powerhouse antenna located on the bay in Texas City. "The Voice of the Mainland," the station called itself. The signal bounced along the entire Gulf of Mexico. Armed with my advertising pamphlets, I called on the station and set out to sell, a poet laureate rhapsodizing and playing my mix of music, just as likely to throw in a white pop song as a black blues record.

Once again I was in over my head.

First thing I didn't realize was the racial complexity of this part of the rural South, especially Louisiana, which the station easily reached. I didn't know that French aristocrats fleeing the French Revolution nearly two centuries before had settled in Louisiana. I didn't know that the Acadians of Nova Scotia, seeking refuge after the British expelled them, had also migrated there. I didn't know about the Creoles, those descendants of the French who were born in Louisiana. I didn't know about the patterns that had developed when all these people mixed with Indians, slaves, and free blacks. I just thought I'd run my mouth and build an audience.

But nothing happened. I wasn't getting the phone calls I was used to getting, and without the phone calls I couldn't play with the listeners, couldn't excite them, couldn't get them to tell their friends about me. My whole being was based on that. A couple of weeks of this and I was so disheartened I was going to give up and look for another station. But then a promoter who booked dances all over the gulf called up and bought an ad, and then he bought another, and pretty soon he was calling me from whatever city he was booking ("I'm in New Iberia. I can hear you! I'm in Abbeville . . .") and I started to plug each little town along Interstate 10, between Lake Charles and Baton Rouge, building a little momentum each day, asking the callers to tell me about their towns. Within a month I was burning in southern Louisiana.

The second thing I didn't realize was that love was approaching.

That's what I got for programming to the females. There wasn't any other R&B radio show where one minute you'd be listening to Joe Turner sing "Honey Hush" (I still remember getting a call from a listener once while that song was playing, and I could hear 'em at home, stomping their feet on the floor) and the next minute you'd be listening to my poetry with a lush Percy Faith instrumental underneath. I knew women liked the husky, confident sound of my voice. They just did. So I didn't think anything of it one afternoon when a couple of teenage girls from Lafayette, Louisiana, one of the bigger towns in my market, a place that got mostly country music on the radio, called up and asked me to play a song. There was a sweetness I liked about one girl's voice, a girl named Rose, and I was delighted when she called in another request soon after.

Now, I'd never gotten involved with a listener, never dated one (whatever I said on the air was part of the performance), but gradually I started dropping Rose's name on the air, started dedicating songs to her—and started making some of the other female callers in some of the other, smaller towns jealous. (There was this one Ray Charles song I kept dedicating to her, and years later, in New York, I was telling this story to Atlantic's Jerry Wexler; he shook his head at a puzzle suddenly solved. "*That's* why that record was so strong out there.") I gave Rose the station's off-air phone number, and we talked a couple more times. Every time I'd learn a little more—just a little. Her age: seventeen. Her last name: Catalon. Where her people came from: France and Catalonia! I was entranced. I was talking to a French girl! Sometimes I'd be spouting my poetry to her and she'd come back with something in French, and she'd laugh, a lighthearted, breathtaking laugh.

On the air, when I got other dedications from Lafayette, I wasn't bashful. I'd ask them: "Do you know Rose Catalon? What does she look like?" And because of the way word got around, the ones who knew her would laugh and go, "Ohhh, you got a live one there!" in that French-accented dialect. To keep their friendship, I'd start dropping their names on the air, too, so that the show sometimes sounded like Lafayette's own station.

That promoter who'd helped me out was listening to all this, and when I told him Rose's age—ten years younger than mine— he cautioned me to watch myself. He was right. This was a shy Catholic-educated teenager. I didn't care. I was already hooked. Rose finally gave me her home phone number, and the more we talked, the more hooked I got. "Describe yourself to me," I said, and little by little she did: not very tall (perfect, because I wasn't, either), red hair, hazel-green eyes. She sounded like the most exotic woman imaginable. This had all started as part of my act, but it wasn't an act any more.

I couldn't keep calling so often, because the station wouldn't keep paying for it and her mother wouldn't tolerate it, but I caught a break. That promoter called to tell me he had a concert set up at the high school in Lafayette. "You wanna emcee it?" he asked. "Not much money but at least you'll get to see that Catalon girl, 'cause it's driving *me* crazy. All the time I drive that highway from Lake Charles to Lafayette it's 'Rose, Rose, Rose.' Now you're talkin' about those areas like you live there. You're naming the streets!"

The show was scheduled for Valentine's Day evening 1955, and before the first band came on, I moved around the room, looking for her. Plenty of girls were coming up, asking for the Great Montague's autograph, but all I did was ask every one of them if they knew where Rose Catalon was. There were other girls with red hair, but I knew they weren't her . . . and then I saw her standing there, laughing and talking. Oh, she'd made no move to find me; she was too reserved to do a thing like that.

"Rose Catalon!" I said, approaching, and I hugged her. We talked. Nothing heavy at all. She was just listening because I was throwing everything I knew at this young lady. I knew this was my shot. I might not get this chance again. I told her about my dreams, the fact that I wouldn't be in Texas much longer, that I was getting ready to go back east and become a star . . . and she listened, starstruck, everybody else standing around her, watching this scene, me still holding her hand while I was talking. I wasn't going to do more than hold her hand—I knew all her friends were going to report everything that happened to their mothers, who'd tell it to Rose's.

"I'm going to call you when I get back," I told her. "But I *am* coming back."

I was in heaven. I kept talking about her on the air. A couple of days later one of the teachers from her school called, a woman who lived in Jennings and listened to the show.

"Your poetry reminds me of Longfellow," she said. "Have you ever heard of *Evangeline*?" Now, I had in fact read some of Longfellow's poetry, like *The Song of Hiawatha* and "Paul Revere's Ride." I remembered reading that and some poetry by Milton when I was as young as ten years old. That romantic poetic part of me ran deep. But *Evangeline* I'd never heard of.

"I'm going to send you a copy," the teacher said. "It's very long. More than a thousand lines. It's a great love story, and I think you may be lovestruck. Maybe you can use some of it on the air, and besides, I think it might be good for the children."

I had no idea how perfectly the stars were aligned in the geography of southern Louisiana. Henry Wadsworth Longfellow had written an epic poem ninety years before dramatizing an ill-fated love affair between Evangeline and Gabriel, who are separated by the French and Indian War. He set it a few miles east of Lafayette, loaded with references to the very region where my heart now beat:

As from a magic trance the sleepers awoke, and the maiden
Said with a sigh to the friendly priest—"O Father Felician!
Something says in my heart that near me Gabriel wanders.
Is it a foolish dream, an idle and vague superstition?
Or has an angel passed, and revealed the truth to my spirit?"
Then, with a blush, she added—"Alas for my credulous fancy!" . . .
"Gabriel truly is near thee [Father Felician said]; for not far away to
    the southward,
On the banks of the Teche are the towns
Of St. Maur and St. Martin.
There the long-wandering bride shall be given again to her
    bridegroom."

After I read the poem, I called Rose and told her I was going to send her a letter. It read like this:

My Evangeline Rose,
You have painted with hazel-green eyes the bayous of your land
And voice sincerely and innocently expressed in melodious
French that made my passion stir.
Who is this Rose that charmed my heart with bliss and laughter,
    ringing bells of excitement in my soul?
A Louisiana queen of Spanish moss and cypress tree.
A miracle and a Cajun dream.
Or is it reminiscences of Evangeline that I see?
Youthful Evangeline traveled from Canada down a raging Mississippi
to Acadian land, looking for her first and only love.
I ask, Dear Rose, have I not traveled miles to find you in this bayou
    land?
It is true that I have been looking to fulfill my romantic imaginations.
I ask, Dear Rose, is it coincidental Evangeline is buried at St.
    Martinville, a few miles from Lafayette, and bequeathed to you
    her romantic feelings?
Could it be underneath the oaks she whispers our names?
But most of all, could it be I love you, my Evangeline Rose?

I mailed it to her. She called me. I thought it would go over her head, but she said it was the most beautiful letter she'd ever received, the most beautiful poem she'd ever heard.

"You love me?" she asked.

"You read the letter, didn't you? I'm coming down to get you. We're going to get married." I had not kissed this girl, had not been alone with her for a moment, but I knew. "I'm taking you out of that town. We're going east. I'll be there in the week."

Actually we were going north. I'd met a guy who'd put together the first Negro radio soap opera. He was syndicating it to different stations. He lived in Chicago, and I was amazed by him because I'd never met a Negro like this: college-educated and debonair, putting on shows like the ones you'd associate with *Days of Our Lives*.

Driving into Lafayette I got into an automobile accident and was hurt badly enough that I had to stay in town overnight—in Rose's house. This was how I met her mother, who was kind enough to let me stay, and we kept our secret until the next day, when we left, drove to Houston, and were married. Best thing that ever happened to me—and I say that after forty-eight years. Rose Catalon would not only love me; she would civilize me, educate me, opening windows of culture I could not dream of. She would, eventually, teach me how to expand the breadth of my collection. She would raise our son and be the glue holding us together. She would endure a nomadic existence as I hop-scotched from one city to another, always looking for a better job, a bigger audience.

She had no idea what she was getting into. I told her we were going to Chicago, but I didn't tell her what it would be like for a teenage white girl to be driving through Texas, Louisiana, Mississippi, and Tennessee with a black man. What did I know? I'd never driven through the South by *myself* before. I didn't paint a picture of hell. I painted a picture of heaven: I'm taking you out of this little town, and I'm gonna be the biggest thing in the world—and she fell for it. I felt bad about hurting her mother's feelings, but I was caught up in my adventure. It was like the tale of Evangeline. She had to follow her love, and so did I, wherever it led. The same way Evangeline searched all over for her love, I found my love. I traveled Texas, through the bayou. I came to get her. You think I'd be warning her about what it was like to be an interracial couple in the South in 1955, warning her that I could get killed just for being with her?

As we traveled, I never got out of the car during the day. I'd drop her off at a coffee shop, let her get a hot meal, and then she'd bring a sandwich in a bag out for me. On the road we'd find a motel—always waiting until after dark—and I'd park a safe distance away from the manager's unit and tell her to go get a room—for herself. Once she was inside the room, I'd hurry in to join her. Same furtive way going out the next morning. But we were never scared. We were having the adventure of our lives. She was two months short of finishing her junior year in high school, laughing and giggling as we began our journey, our discovery of life and each other. Even then there was something deep down inside of her that was all woman, that let her take on those responsibilities.

We passed one billboard that said, "Run, Nigger, Run. Don't let the sun go down on you." In Memphis we stayed in a blacks-only place, the Lorraine Motel, on whose balcony Doctor King would spend his last moments. I anticipated Chicago would become the place I finally exploded and found fame. And while that would be true, Chicago became even more memorable to me because of an accidental stumbling into an obscure bookstore and an even more obscure book.

One of my first jobs: in the furniture store broadcasting remotely during a brief stint on KFOX in Long Beach, California, in 1952.

On the air in Chicago, 1955.

On the air with Louis Jordan, 1956, selling for sponsors.

Certificate of conversion to Judaism, St. Louis, 1960.

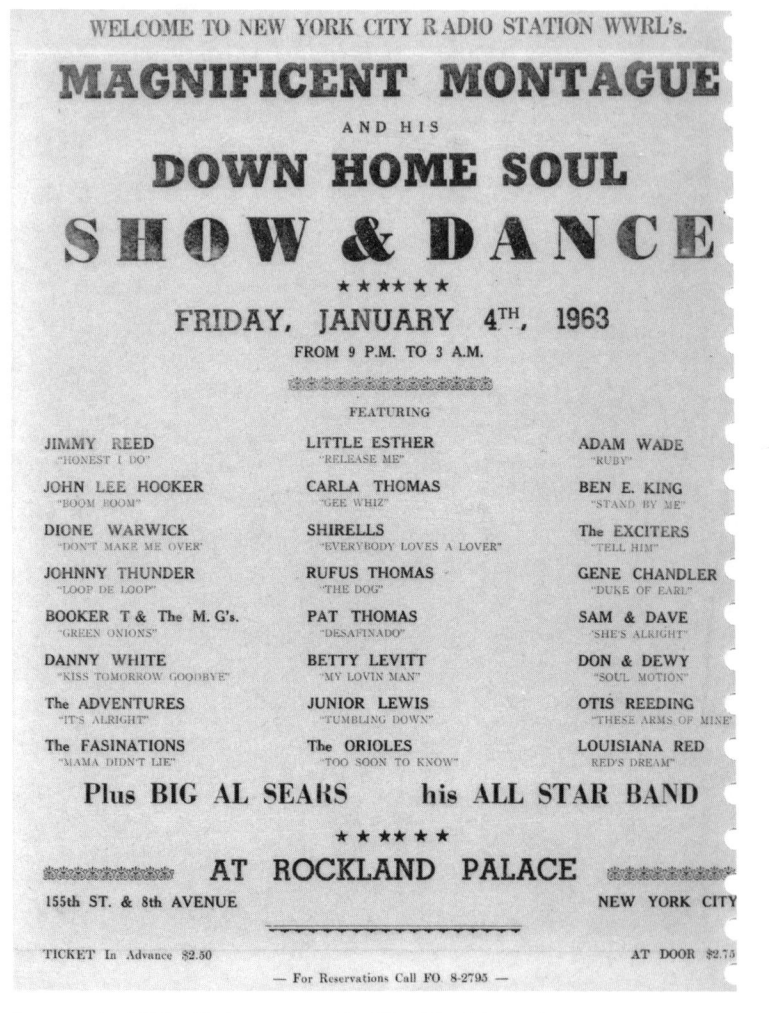

I promoted this all-star concert in New York in 1963.

Clowning on my bongo drums, Los Angeles, 1965.

With Rose at Martin's high school graduation in Los Angeles, 1973.

In the studio of the Palm Springs radio station Rose and I built, 1985.
(*Los Angeles Times* photo by Marsha Trager)

4 The Book

It happened in a secondhand book-store on Halsted Street in a Jewish area of Chicago, spring of '56.

I was shopping for poetry after finishing my 6–9 A.M. show on WAAF, the big white radio station owned by the people who owned the stockyards. I liked to mix in other poets with the original verse I read to "my darlings" on the air. I was leafing through a book of poems by Omar Khayyám when, underneath it, I spotted something by Paul Laurence Dunbar. He was nothing but a name to me, but the owner of the shop said: "You ought to buy that book. It's great musical dialect."

I didn't know what he was talking about, but I bought it anyway, drove back to my little office, turned to a page and—damn! What *was* this?

> G'way an' quit dat noise, Miss Lucy,
> Put dat music book away;
> What's de use to keep on tryin'?

Ef you practise twell you're gray,
You cain't sta't no notes a-flyin'
Lak de ones dat rants and rings
Fom de kitchen to de big woods
When Malindy sings.

Never had I read words that sounded so raw, so real, so different. To fashion my mind, my mouth, around these words was like time travel; they connected me to the generations that spawned me. In the light of today's modern times, maybe you find them off-putting, too reminiscent of the way we are mocked. I was too mystified by what I was reading to wonder. At first I assumed these were the transcriptions of an uneducated sharecropper. Nothing had prepared me for the truth: Paul Laurence Dunbar had lived a brief, brilliant life. He was "pure black"—neither parent had white ancestors. His father had escaped from slavery in Kentucky to Canada, and his mother came to Ohio after the Civil War. His parents loved literature, his high school classmates and friends (Dayton Central, class of 1890) were the Wright brothers, and by age twenty-one Dunbar was being published. Within a few years he won a national reputation as the greatest Negro poet since two Europeans with black blood, Aleksandr Sergeyevich Pushkin, the Russian poet whose great-grandfather was the general Abraham Hannibal, and the elder Alexandre Dumas, the French author of *The Three Musketeers,* whose grandmother was black. On this day, a half-century after Dunbar's death, all I knew was that I was bent over a poem I could not stop reading:

You ain't got de nachel o'gans
Fu' to make de soun' come right,
You ain't got de tu'ns an' twistin's
Fu' to make it sweet an' light.
Tell you one thing now, Miss Lucy,
An' I'm tellin' you fu' true,
When hit comes to raal right singin',
'Tain't no easy thing to do.

I felt a rare moment of furious racial pride, much like I had felt when I saw Paul Robeson speak: this is us, the elemental sound of Negro people, the voice that separates us, defines us, distinguishes us. As I leafed through the poems, I was surprised to see that Dunbar was not limited to dialect poetry. There was another voice— deeper, contemporary. Do you remember that expression I told you a couple chapters back: "We wear the mask"? It was on this afternoon in Chicago that I read that poem for the first time. Its conclusion is hauntingly transcendent:

> We smile, but, O great Christ, our cries
> To thee from tortured souls arise.
> We sing, but oh the clay is vile
> Beneath our feet, and long the mile;
> But let the world dream otherwise,
> We wear the mask!

I knew by this point in my life that I was an artist, but I think this was the first time I as a reader had felt the power of a great artist speaking to my soul, felt the magic recognition that there must be more, there had to be more of his work. Two weeks later I was out scouting. I walked into a beautiful scholarly book shop with fine editions and high prices, and the proprietor looked at me with a curious eye.

"Are you a collector?"

"Yes," I said with false confidence. "I'm looking for Paul Laurence Dunbar."

He walked me over to the shelf at the east of the store. "This is all Dunbar. My personal collection. These books are rare." I was puzzled. I didn't know what was coming next. "I'm asking eighteen hundred dollars for the lot."

Well, I damn near went through the ceiling. I was making maybe $100 a week. But two hours later, having emptied my meager savings, I was back with the cash and walked out with my first meaningful volume, the first of thousands of purchases of the black experience, the first of tens of thousands of journeys into book-

stores and thrift shops and barns and antique stores looking for
literature, biographies, art, posters, and lithos, skimming whole
periodicals to find one line, a word, about the Negro—looking for
that word, or *nigger,* or *colored,* or *blacks*—to tell me something new
about slavery, or our contributions, or achievements . . . this was
the first symptom of that virus. Thank you, Mister Dunbar, for the
fire you lit inside me. Rose thought I was crazy, but my young soul
rejoiced, and it wasn't too long before Dunbar extended his
hold . . . to my radio show.

He collided with an elemental blues singer named Jimmy Reed,
a kindred spirit who knew nothing of him yet shared his spirit.
Soon, and probably to the bafflement of many of my listeners, I was
layering together these two voices, a half-century apart: reciting
Dunbar's dialect poetry rather than my own and then segueing into
Jimmy: "Ain't That Lovin' You, Baby," or "Big Boss Man," or "You
Don't Have to Go." I was captivated by how both men's art came
from the same plain, powerful, slurred southern voice. I started
playing them together so much that Vivian and Jimmy Bracken,
who owned Jimmy's record company, Vee Jay, started asking, "Is
there a verse there that Jimmy is doing we don't know about?"

This metaphysical encounter could only have happened—let
alone succeeded on the air—in Chicago, and probably only in the
midfifties. Over the previous ten years another huge Negro migration from the South had been pushing its way here, two thousand
new black faces a week abandoning the plantations for the steel
mills. If I told you I'd made a calculated move there from Texas, if
I told you I knew that Chicago would be the perfect laboratory for
my talent, I'd be lying. I went there for the same reason every ambitious jockey or actor or sharecropper moves, the same reason that
would push me from city to city so many times in the next decade:
a bigger market, a bigger stage, a better chance at freeing what was
inside me.

The black migration made Chicago a magnet for R&B talent, a
breeding ground for the melodies of southern country blues and
the electrified rhythms of northern blues musicians. It also made

Chicago the birthplace of a dozen independent record companies that gambled on being able to feed that hungry Negro marketplace, all of them cluttered on South Michigan Avenue with names like Chess, Chance, King, Constellation, Brunswick . . . , and most important to me, a two-year-old company called Vee Jay, which in these years before the success of Motown would become the most financially successful black-owned record company.

Vee Jay was the label of Jimmy Reed, Gene Chandler, the Impressions, the Dells—and the Beatles. (Vee Jay had the Beatles locked up in U.S. distribution rights in '62 when Capitol didn't want them; it put out one album and held onto them for a year before the lawyers descended and snatched 'em back.) Vee Jay was the first black record company that was able to cross over and deal with white power brokers like Dick Clark. It was the company that taught me about writing and publishing. It was the first company I saw booking black acts at white venues. Its story is a tribute to that quality of greatness you always read about in accounts of people from the other side of the tracks who make it—that gift of being too dumb to know what you shouldn't be able to do.

The *Vee* in Vee Jay stood for Vivian Carter Bracken, who was a deejay in Gary, Indiana, and also ran a record store. Around the time I was getting off that ship in Galveston, it was dawning on Vivian that she could be her own record supplier, her own company. So she and her husband, Jimmy, who was the *Jay* and who was running a shoe-shine business, borrowed a few hundred dollars and started looking for artists—blues, gospel, and a style that would later be known as doo-wop.

One of the first singers they ran into was a blues-playing steelworker in Gary, up from Mississippi, sounding like your mushmouth, countrified grandfather, slow and deliberate—but let him play his mouth harp and put his old friend Eddie Taylor's electric boogie-rhythm guitar behind him and . . . damn, Jimmy Reed was something. He was the kind of singer, the kind of artist, who grabbed listeners with his primitiveness. No matter what city I was working, my listeners could never get enough of him, the same way they could never get enough of Ray Charles or Otis Redding eight or ten years later. There was something in the voice that was so authentic, so down-home, something that touched northern black listeners with a sense of where they'd come from, the way something in Dunbar touched the same nerve in me.

Bronzeville was what Negroes called our piece of Chicago. I thought I was going back north from Texas, period, but I didn't know the history of this place. I didn't know that the man credited with founding Chicago was black: Jean Baptiste Point Du Sable, one of hundreds of Negroes who settled in the Mississippi Valley in the eighteenth century, a Haitian who erected the first house in Chicago in 1779. I didn't know about the 1919 Chicago race war, forged by the bitterness of European immigrants at the surging black population and erupting with the drowning of a black boy at a bathing beach, resulting in the deaths of twenty Negroes and fourteen whites. The invisible stains were still there: when you wanted to go to the beach, you went down to Lakeshore Drive and you didn't see any signs, you just saw us. If there were a thousand Negroes, they were grouped in one space, not spread all over; that's where you knew to go. It was understood: if you wanted to stay alive, you didn't go out of that area. I wasn't ready for it. Anybody who tells you they're ready is a bullshit liar. I wasn't angry. You didn't ask no questions to your brothers and sisters out there. You knew why they were huddled up there. We didn't talk like that. That's where they put you, so that's where you had to go. If someone did veer across, that's when a riot started—with all the black policemen we had, with all the power in the black wards, it still didn't matter. There was less freedom there than in the South, really, because we did not know where the oppression was coming from. In the South the lines were drawn by signs or partitions. Here you simply knew not to go into the Polish neighborhood or get lost in the Irish neighborhood. You knew to be a good navigator. You wore the mask.

But I'd come here to work and I was working. Right after Rose and I rolled into town in the spring of '55, I walked into WGES and introduced myself to the Ole Swingmaster, Al Benson, a Negro broadcasting legend who'd started out as a radio preacher in the midforties but became so successful as a deejay that he was on the air seven or eight hours a day within a couple of years. By the late forties a *Chicago Tribune* poll voted Benson the city's most popular jockey—ahead of the leading whites. He was Mississippi-born, a soul-to-soul connection with the city's new black arrivals.

"Take care of my records," Benson told me, and for two or three weeks that's what I did, acting as his gofer, carrying the records he needed or picked up as he made his way through the station and the city. I gradually found a way to sell some time and get on the mike on WGES. There were no black-oriented radio stations in Chicago, simply individual shows. But I got lucky: a black jockey on a big middle-of-the-road station, WAAF, died, and a white jockey there named Marty Fay (who within a few months would start breaking rock 'n' roll records on the air to protest that new, dangerous style) got in touch with me. We worked out a deal where I started brokering a little time each day, and from there I started growing, playing that Montague mix of soul and white pop, reaching out to "my darlings," until I owned the morning in Chicago. This didn't surprise me; I'd been flipping my car radio dial when we first drove in, and the jockeys were flat. Before I even had a job, I had funeral wreaths delivered to the morning jockeys on the other stations from the Great Montague.

The top morning guy in Chicago was Howard "Moo Moo" Miller on WMAQ, playing Mitch Miller, that kind of fluff. I obliterated him on WAAF, and in the process I found a more sophisticated, alliterative nickname to set myself apart from the pack: Magnificent Montague.

I was magnificent not merely by coming strong with Ray Charles and Muddy Waters and Otis Rush and Jimmy Reed but by exploiting my personal quirks. First, I was the only Negro jockey on this station, and while I sometimes broadcast with Negro fervor, I wasn't trying to "sound" black. I wasn't saying, "Co'mon, y'all!" I have a distinctive northern feel to my voice, an elegant sort of haughtiness. There were black deejays on the air in Chicago who you knew right off were black: "Open up your icebox, pull up yo' orange crate, we gonna git down. We gonna get the chitlins out, baby!" That wasn't me. I was playing Jimmy Reed, but I was also playing Fats Domino and Dinah Washington—artists whites loved, too, especially the white kids who were just beginning to cross over. Second, I was reading my own poetry mixed over lush organ arrangements, reaching out to the women ("My darlings, did you know that today on the bus on State I saw a man sitting while one of my darlings was standing?"), and just like in Texas, it was causing a certain consternation on the part of white listeners to hear a white lady call up my show, tell me what part of town she lived in, and ask me to dedicate one of my poems to her. (It was also causing me to be confronted on the street by more than one resentful boyfriend.) I was flying on instinct, and it was working—primarily because most everybody else on the air knew the rules and had a stake in obeying them.

The fact that I didn't care about the rules was the reason I started mixing Dunbar and Jimmy Reed together on the air. They blurred so much in my mind that I was shocked when I realized that Jimmy was only two years older than me! He was thirty-one then, but he sounded like sixty-two, like he could have been a contemporary of Dunbar's. He was Dunbar in rhythm. Finally I understood what that bookseller meant by "great musical dialect."

It never occurred to me to worry that most of Jimmy's fans never heard of Dunbar, and vice versa. It never occurred to me to worry that in that modern era, the light-skinned Negro elite who looked down on colored folks as colored as me might find Dunbar's dialect embarrassing. If I'd fallen in love with his words, I knew others would, too. They were elegant! They were culture! (And damn hard to write; back yourself up a couple pages and try reading a few lines aloud—you'll see.) I knew, too, that whites *loved* dialect poetry—they'd flocked to Br'er Rabbit and all the folk stories of the South. Dunbar's first works had been printed in white magazines; readers didn't have any clue he was black until a white poet decided to help Dunbar get his first book published while Dunbar was working as an elevator operator in Ohio. The tragedy was that neither Montague nor his father knew a darn thing about Dunbar. We didn't know our own contributions.

Watching Jimmy Reed in the studio was part of the greatest feeling in the world: watching unschooled black artists put together music and lyrics. Watching and listening to talent off the street, fresh out of the factory or school or from the storefront churches—a combination of God-given talent, no music charts, no paper or head-up arrangements—watching them changing keys in their head, cutting down the time of a song from their heart, mouthing all the instrumental parts 'cause they can't play the instrument, instinctively translating a thousand moments of church singing to build the right R&B feel, then standing back and listening to the new creation. It was the thrill of watching a singing group plot a tune that was never really completed at rehearsal, seeing 'em run through three or four mediocre takes, take a break, go to the bathroom, send out for some food, sit around accusing each other of stepping on each other's notes, then take the last verse, make it the opening line, cut the last eight bars, find a new gimmick—and make it work on the next take. Jimmy Reed would do two, three takes of "Honest I Do" in the studio, and Vee Jay would pick the third and ask him to do it again, and Jimmy couldn't do it the same way—he'd forgotten what he did. Jimmy would do it every time with a slight little something he created. Vivian would have Jimmy's wife whisper the lyrics back to him in his ear, and he'd sing the next line. When it was over, they'd say, "Jimmy, sing it again," and he'd sing it *another* way. Then he'd go on the road and they'd send him a tape so he could learn the song he'd cut. And it worked, somehow. Magic.

It was a short leap from Dunbar to other distant voices. They were all there, in bookstores, all of them private history lessons, all of them waiting for me, and me hungry for them all. The discovery of Dunbar had stirred a simple, powerful question: what else was out there that nobody had told me about? I was at an age, and my race was at a point in its history, at which I felt myself pulled toward fundamental questions. Who were we? What had shaped us? How did this happen, this nebulous existence in which we were not slaves yet not free? I didn't wake up each day asking myself these questions, but to be in Chicago, on the cusp of the modern civil rights movement, was to feel them nonetheless, hanging in the air like dense snow clouds.

Obsessed with setting myself apart from normal radio, I started using some of the musty books and magazines I was beginning to buy to create a little five-minute weekly spot, a historical tidbit called "They Paved the Way." White announcers had their discussion programs—Mike Wallace was big in Chicago for doing just that—and general-market stations had their editorials and commentaries and public-service segments to meet FCC requirements. But I was the first black deejay to come up with a musical mix incorporating historical talk. Since I was brokering the ads and paying for my time, the station didn't give a damn what I did, so every so often I'd pull the needle off the end of, say, B. B. King's "3 O'Clock Blues" and announce something like:

THEY PAVED THE WAY! (Dramatic music up.) The scene is Richmond of 1800. Abroad the French Revolution is winding down. At home Thomas Jefferson is proclaiming his disturbing ideas about democracy. In Haiti Toussaint L'Ouverture has ousted the French and British and is setting up his kingdom of blacks. (Dramatic music up.) Stagecoaches roll over dusty trails out West. Southern crackers sniff their snuff and sip mint juleps while their slaves pick cotton in the hot sun. (Dramatic music up even higher.) Then from a clear sky comes what startles Richmond out of its complacency, shocks it into an alarmed reaction. The unthinkable has come to pass: the slaves have revolted. They fight slave catchers and flee, hiding in trees and swamps, escaping aboard wagons. A group of teenage boys and girls, determined to be free, surrounded by a posse, stand their ground and, armed with a double-barreled pistol and a knife, fearlessly refuse to retreat an inch and drive off the slave catchers. Aided by the underground railroad, they reach Philadelphia safely. *They* paved the way.

There was tumult in the air—the birth of the modern civil rights movement—that made these spots more poignant: in the summer of '55 a Chicago boy named Emmett Till was murdered in Mississippi by whites who believed he'd made a pass at a white woman, and his killers were swiftly acquitted. In December an Alabama woman named Rosa Parks refused to give up her seat on the bus to a white man, triggering a year-long Negro boycott that introduced America to Martin Luther King. "What was the slave?" my Chicago listeners would hear me wonder aloud, and then I'd read my own description:

> Here was sorrow hardened as steel, carved on a black man's face. Here was a body on which the "for sale" sign branded them like cattle, cut out the soul, made them property. Here was unholy sadness eating out a black man's heart. What was it like? Here was a mother, stripped naked, body and soul, pleading, begging, clinging in desolation: "Oh, Massa, don't take my child." Here was a race singing in the wilderness: "Lord, deliver me. You helped Daniel, you helped Moses, too; Lord, let my people go." Here was a race that endured all the sufferings. Here was sadness carved on a black man's face, the branding iron of a parasite civilization, burning a soul. Should not a soul sing of joy? Should not a soul sing of peace? You, my listeners are a part of that soul.

Often I simply went with a piece from my collection that grabbed me. Imagine how this quotation, which I found in a 1917 issue of a black music magazine (whose very existence I found stunning), captured the imagination of a Negro music audience:

> Antonin Dvorak was a famous Czech composer. He featured in his "New World Symphony" the Negro spirituals, "Swing Low, Sweet Chariot," "Somebody Is Knocking," and "Roll, Jordan, Roll." To Dvorak, our pentatonic melody, a musical scale

without the fourth and seventh step, was perfectly familiar, innate in Czechoslovakian songs and dances. Dvorak, after directing the National Conservatory of Music in New York in the late 1890s and touring America, publicly declared: "The future of this country must be founded upon what are called the Negro melodies. This must be the real foundation of any serious and original school of composition to be developed in the United States. These are the folk songs of America and your composers must turn to them. Beethoven's most charming *scherzo* is based upon what might be considered a skillfully handled Negro melody. In Negro melodies is found all that is needed for a great and noble school of music. They are pathetic, tender, passionate melodies, solemn, religious, bold, merry, gay or what you will. It is music that suits itself to any mood or purpose. The Negro in America utters a new note full of sweetness and as characteristic as any music of any country."

You can do anything you want on radio if you remember that you must paint a picture for the audience. Radio is film of the mind, and if you understand drama—which also means anticipating boredom—your listeners will follow you anywhere. I didn't just play a record. Since I understood music, I knew to blend songs whose keys matched or complemented each other, whose lyrics did not overlap thematically, whose storylines and melodies were different. If I had a record with an instrumental that I thought was too long, I'd go into the studio and take four bars out. If I had another record I dug, and it was 2:40 long, I might take another copy of the record and have it cued up on a second turntable so I could extend the instrumental break. The other deejays were horrified— how dare I? Staff announcers were ordered to play tight records. But I wasn't a staff announcer; I couldn't have cared less. This was for my audience. (Decades later somebody would "invent" the EP single.) Problem was, of course, people started walking into record stores complaining that what they'd bought didn't sound like what they'd heard on the radio. "You're not helping us, Montague," the record companies would complain, and there were times when push came to shove and the record company gave in, pulled the record, and rerecorded it to my specs. They didn't like it, and God knows there were other places in Chicago they could have gotten airplay on their own terms, but they couldn't get the Magnificent Montague rhapsody—the poetry, the introduction, and *then* the song.

One day I got a record, a ballad, and the lead singer sounded just like my old boyhood pal and Merchant Marine companion Tony Williams, who I'd lost track of. It had "hit" written all over it, passionate and dreamy at the same time. Tony had been discovered in '54 by a producer named Buck Ram, who put him together with some other boys as lead singer and recorded a song called "Only You." Tony and his group, the Platters, passed through Chicago a couple weeks after I heard the record and visited the station. He said, "When I hear you introduce 'Only You' in Chicago, you—" and I knew where he was going. "I take you back to church," I said. "Yeah," he said, "because you do the sermon first."

That same year Syd Nathan, the founder of King Records, calls me about a song, sends me a dub, tells me he's afraid it's a piece of shit because the singer is stuttering one word over and over. I listen and I laugh at his stupidity, because this is a church record to end all church records. I sure as hell know how to sell this one because it opens with the singer's voice, no instruments, allowing me to bump my spoken introduction right up against it, bang-bang. "Darlings," I said, "what*ever* you do, don't give your man a second chance until he screams, 'Please! Please! Please!'"—and in the next half-second James Brown screamed that immortal plea, screamed just the way they plead for redemption, when they plead for you to come before the church and give up your sin, when they plead for you to ask the Lord to forgive you and take you. "Please, Lord, please, Lord, I want to go to heaven." It was frightening how fast the phone lines lit up when that record went on. I might be playing it on a Wednesday at 7:30 A.M., but J. B. took 'em two other places at once: a lonely apartment at 2 P.M. Saturday and a crowded church at 10 A.M. Sunday, reaffirming the fact that in soul music there was only a hair difference between the expressions "I need you, Jesus" and "I need you, baby."

Gradually "They Paved the Way" became a sponsored show. I'd take three or four black mom-and-pop businesses in Chicago that couldn't afford to buy a block of time direct from the station and ask them to each pay me something small, $10 a week apiece. I had three shows like that a week, which meant I always had ten to fifteen small businesses on the air that wouldn't have been there otherwise.

I had to know these businesses, just like I had to know the black record companies. There was an intimate relationship between the jockeys and the independent labels—there had to be, simply for survival on both ends. Somebody wants to call it a conflict of interest, or payola—whatever, fine with me. That's the vocabulary of the ruling class, and back in the day we ruled nothing. I might be making $50 or $100 a week on the air, no matter how famous I might have sounded or seemed. So when Vee Jay or Chess called me and asked me to come down to a prerecording session to hear one of their young men sing, I knew a consulting fee went along with it. I didn't sit around sobbing about how a Negro couldn't make a full-time living on the air, or how he couldn't join the announcer's union. What good's that going to do? The system—more accurately, I guess, the lack of any system—worked to my advantage. I knew I had a good ear and a good mouth and that I could eventually record or produce records as good as the ones I was deciding to play. It made me see the business in a broader light.

Say a record company had a hot record and wanted me to put it on my playlist. I'd say, hey, my deal is simple. I have a relationship with a couple of record shops in town that advertise on my block of radio time, and you have promotional records (which we call free goods). Send me $300 in free goods and I'll get them promoted in the record stores (which would pay me for the records), and I'll play the record on my show. And that's legal. I didn't have to say, "Gimme $100 for a one-time shot."

Or if you sent me a record, and I was lucky enough to have a big beer company as a sponsor, I'd go into a liquor store in a black neighborhood and use that to barter for better shelf position for my sponsor. Now, most of these stores are owned by whites, so I go looking for that black guy behind the counter, or maybe the assistant manager, and I tell him: "Gimme shelf position and order twenty-five cases above your norm. I'll take care of you. Just lemme come in and take a picture and show my sponsor I'm doing merchandising beyond my show." I'd do that at maybe five black outlets in Chicago. Now, I wasn't making enough money to take care of any of the sons of bitches myself, so I'd call back the record company that sent me the record and say: "You sent me no. 1939 and it's a dog, but you guys seem to think it's gonna be great one day, so I'll play it if you send me 100 copies." I'd take the 100 copies into a friendly record shop and convert 'em into records that those liquor store assistant managers liked—jazz, classical, whatever—to pay 'em back for shelf position.

Or sometimes it'd work this way. The record company would have a dub—a test pressing of the master—and send it to me to ask me what my ear said. (By the time I got on the air in New York in the early sixties, Atlantic and Motown would be doing this constantly.) I'd say, "That's pretty good, but you gotta pump up the bridge," or, "the opening is too tepid"—you get the idea. "Now, if you use it," I'd tell 'em, "I want a piece of the publishing rights. Or I want a piece of the writing credit." That happened anytime you changed anything.

Then it was up to me to make the record happen. Sure, I had an investment in it, but I only invested in a record I knew had the power to work on the air. Thing was, you couldn't just break a record by playing it over and over. You had to get out in the community. You had to get out there and do your record hops. You had to have a remote show at a club or a teen post and come up with something so you could spin it and spin it and talk and talk. The hops were a barometer, more so than the phone calls you'd get when you were on the air. Sometimes I'd run out of records and start playing the B sides and discover *there* was the real hit.

I had to be a full-time personality and a take-charge, juggling-a-bunch-of-balls businessman. Which is how I *got* that big beer company—Budweiser—I was using as a hypothetical example a minute ago.

Now, it wasn't a big deal to be a deejay and have Budweiser ads on your show, but I wanted to be Budweiser's black voice in Chicago, and at this point Budweiser already had a lone paid (white) voice: Howard Miller, my archenemy on WMAQ. I was also convinced Budweiser would be better off if I wrote my own ad copy, and no deejay of any color had done that; Bud's ad agency would never go for it. So I made an appointment to see the old man himself, August Anheuser Busch Jr., in St. Louis, and I told him how he could be number one with black Chicago if he bought the Montague show on my terms. He told me he already had a fine deejay as spokesman in Chicago, but he also told me he did indeed care about the black market, which to his company's credit was true. I looked him in the eye and said: "Mr. Busch, pay me a third of what you pay that white guy, and I will give you what it takes to make the market right. But with that, I'd like to have the autonomy to work directly with Budweiser's black salesmen, to offer marketing giveaways and promotional items to small mom-and-pop retail outlets, to work hand in hand with black-owned nightclubs, and to produce my own theme songs with Budweiser in them." I also told him he'd need to put blacks on his billboards.

And damned if he didn't go for it: a fifteen-minute spot, renewable every thirty days, reporting to Bud's Chicago branch office. See, Gussie Busch was smarter than the other beer merchants. He was spending far more money for advertising, and for the first time he'd passed Schlitz in '55 to become the country's top-selling beer. I threw myself into this opportunity, took as many free goods as I could get my hands on from record companies, and used them to run promotions in more than 100 black retail outlets that sold Budweiser. I came up with my own Budweiser Chicago slogan—"Take Five! Come alive with Budweiser!"—and held giveaway after giveaway on "Budweiser Montague" days. It was the start of a corporate relationship that continued no matter what city I worked in.

But the best hustle, while not the most enriching one, came from emceeing a talent show at Hyde Park High late in '55. The winners, a doo-wop group of four kids called the Tams (they didn't have money for uniforms, so they wore tam-o'-shanters), caught my ear. There was another jockey around town, Herb "the Kool Gent" Kent, who had a young singing group he named the Kool Gents, and when I saw the Tams, I figured I'd swipe his idea—but I never figured my first toe in the water would sell half a million records.

"You boys," I told the lead singer, Johnny Keyes, "are no longer the Tams. You are the Magnificents, and we are going to make a record." And from that day forth, those boys hung on for dear life. I had them at the radio station almost every day, either singing on the air or practicing in one of the little studios. Meanwhile I was writing their hit record—how could it *not* be a hit when (a) I was writing and arranging it, (b) my relationship with Vee Jay demanded they put the record out, and (c) my show and my marketing connections were so strong that practically every breathing person Chicago was eventually going to hear this song? It helped that Johnny and the boys were so green, because they put up with me pushing them through the most hellish rehearsals.

What I wrote (giving half the writing credit to Vee Jay's general manager, Ewart Abner, because that's how you greased things) was a hybrid. It was to have the standard doo-wop harmonies, emphasizing Johnny's tenor and Willie Myles's bass line, but to be sung faster, with a churchy feel, a double-kick drumbeat. Think of the fastest song a black church choir is gonna sing on Sunday morning and add a doo-wop feel. Got that?

Don't feel bad, nobody else seemed to get it at first, either.

We went into Universal Recording Studios in January '56, and it was the first time the boys had ever seen a tape recorder, let alone tried to work this precisely with musicians. (That was the beauty of doo-wop in the first place, right? All you were supposed to need was the right acoustics in the boys' tiled bathroom at school. The voices were the instruments.) So with Vivian and Jimmy Bracken watching, we moved through unsatisfying take after unsatisfying take.

When you're self-taught, you come with ideas that look totally strange and backward to a polished composer, but the soul feeling (Johnny Keyes reminds me that I was the first person he heard use the word *soul*) compensates. I'd develop my lyrics while beating on my conga and bongo drums for rhythms. I'd play my accordion, developing the melody with the right hand keys of the instrument.

I called the Magnificents' first song "Up on the Mountain" and told Johnny to sing this:

> *Well, I went up on the mountain one bright and early morn*
> *And I fell down on my knees and then I sang a song:*
> *Oh darlin', my little darlin', hear my plea, don't leave me . . .*

The tempo didn't change, but now the bass came in, solo:

> *I'm gonna sing, yes, I'm gonna shout*
> *About the girl who broke my heart*

Then out of nowhere the band skids to a quick stop, and you hear Johnny, with no backing:

> *Why did you leave me?*
> *Why did you go and say good-bye?*

And then the band starts up again for the second stanza. But as the song moved along it grew complex, because I heard in my head a one-time refrain where the band fell silent again and those doo-wop voices soared at once ("She took my money uh-*huhhhh* . . .") and then kicked back into that churchy rhythm, finishing off with an intricate ending in which the singer recounts all the love wounds he has suffered—all of it jammed into 2:47. Of course I have this all in my head and not written down anywhere, and I have to either find the words to explain it to the musicians and the singers or sit there and try to play or sing all the parts myself. I chose the latter.

(Johnny remembers the phrase, "Okay, if I have to I'm gonna sing this motherfucker myself!" being used on a number of occasions.)

What drove everybody crazy was the rhythm I was going for, something like the way the double handclap in church drives a song, mixed with the basic foundation of jubilee singing: the piano one beat behind the vocal and the drum a beat behind the piano. The session drummer, a jazz drummer who read music, threatened to quit, saying he couldn't do it. "Listen to me!" I shouted, and I did the drum part with my mouth, doing all the parts, acting like a nut. Twenty minutes later they got it.

I knew "Up on the Mountain" would be a regional hit, but it did far better, making the national R&B Top 10, at that point the biggest seller ever for Vee Jay. Like everything I did, this was a bridge to another hustle. The Magnificents were a snack and I wanted a meal—somebody I could build into a star. I seized upon the Cooke family of Chicago, which had already produced one gospel superstar: Sam Cooke. In '56 Sam was a year away from busting out as a pop singer, but he had a younger brother, L. C., with a great word-of-mouth reputation forged from singing with every gospel group that passed through Chicago. L. C. had never been recorded. So in the summer of '56 I drove my new Mercury convertible to the Cooke house, introduced myself to L. C., and—with the carefully won approval of his father, Charles, a bishop in the Church of Christ Holiness Church—signed the young man up as another of the Magnificents. I had no illusions about the group going far. They were one-hit wonders riding my coattails; talent-wise, none of 'em could hold a candle to L. C.'s pent-up, harshly beautiful voice. I added a female lead, Barbara Arrington, and soon the group was playing the Apollo and the rest of the chitlin circuit, but I gradually lost interest and began producing L. C. as a solo artist on Chess. Not only did L. C. have the Cooke gift of song, but he was a powerful songwriter. He penned two hits, "Do You Remember?" and "Blue Tears," that are still selling today. Johnny Keyes kept the group's name with my blessing and has been performing with an evolving squad of Magnificents at oldies shows ever since.

It was in Chicago that I heard, and met, Elvis Presley, and felt that stab of ambivalence I have never gotten over. First time I heard one of Elvis's records I said this man *must* have been raised by blacks. It was that obvious. And during that breakout year of his, '56, when he was on every network TV show and visiting all us jockeys as he toured, he was the same way everybody says, polite and respectful, aware of how dependent his career had been on the feel and the style of black music. You wanted to say this is one white boy we don't have to worry about.

And yet, no matter how nice he was, you still felt knifed in the back. A part of you felt robbed, violated. They'd beaten you again. Look, here I was in a northern city where, just a few months previous, I'd hosted a promotional appearance by Fats Domino at a record shop on State Street, downtown, and the only way I could do it was by agreeing to have separate hours for black and white kids to come down there. This was a time when as soon as Fats Domino put out "Ain't That a Shame," another record company rushed out a soulless note-for-note cover version by a white college English major named Pat Boone. We'd seen the white Crewcuts cover the Chords' "Sh-Boom" in '54. We'd seen the white Georgia Gibbs cover Lavern Baker's "Tweedlee Dee" in '55 and, that same year, cover Etta James's "Roll with Me Henry." We'd seen the white Bill Haley make a hit out of Big Joe Turner's "Shake, Rattle, and Roll." Every time, it was like having it rubbed in your face: black labels weren't paying shit royalties to begin with, and now the white companies were going to co-opt what little we had. Practically before we got it out of our mouths, they took it. (By '57, it would get even worse, because the master robber, Dick Clark, would take his *American Bandstand* TV show nationwide, play those cover versions, and make sure you didn't see many black faces—particularly on his dance floor.) You wonder why black folk talk about conspiracies where white people don't see them? This was one: a conspiracy to sell black music to whites by making it look white and never tell the consumer where it came from. Some of those black artists would be dead before the next generation of white artists—the first generation with a conscience, bands like the Rolling Stones—gave credit where credit was due.

Which is why many Negroes watched the rise of Elvis Presley with a sick feeling in our stomachs. It reminded us how little of the process we owned. (A few years down the road, Lloyd Price would shock the business by having the foresight to demand control of his publishing—having the nerve to claim legal control of the songs he wrote rather than sign it away to a record company for a few pennies. That would be viewed as a revolutionary act! That's the kind of plantation we grew up on.) We saw white deejays all over the country popularizing black music, making more money, taking more payola, and getting more than black deejays. We saw, too, that the bigger Elvis got, the more racial resentment flared up against us—had you seen any backlash demonstrations by whites against "nigger music" before Elvis got on TV? We thought, too, about all the white artists we'd met who'd said, sincerely, how much they loved black music, how they'd like to wake up one morning and be colored. And we'd think be careful what you wish for, son; it doesn't wash off. (None of this would prepare me, a decade later, for something even cruder: the rise of Wolfman Jack, who'd come to L.A. in '65, the same year I was king of black radio there, and tried to steal everything but my underwear. Wolfman, blacking up his face with makeup, stealing Howlin' Wolf's dialect, putting on his wig, going out and growling like a twentieth-century minstrel. He was, to his evil credit, the best of the white imitators—talking Negro, acting Negro, getting loud to draw a crowd —and he fooled some people for a while, because he was pimping the greatest music ever made, mid-1960s soul music, to back up his act. And how can you argue with the results? He became a cult figure and then a legend. He simply didn't do it, if anyone's keeping score, on his own talent.)

Elvis had to get outside himself to succeed. He had to pretend to be black. He had to pretend to have it in his soul. He needed to adopt Negro characteristics and idiosyncrasies to reproduce his own talent with the gift of black folk. Elvis said he learned the blues from colored folks, but what price did he pay? Did he love us enough to find a way to get some of those royalties back into the hands of the impoverished black writers and singers he copied? Is it too harsh to raise that moral obligation? Elvis gets his due from white folk, but he's not gonna get anything from me. The money, fame, and fortune are still overdue to his sources. As Elvis and the rest of those white imitators have journeyed to white musical heaven, I have no doubt they've heard some sounds they recognize coming from next door—that shoutin', that hand-clappin', that singin'. That's black musical heaven. I know the white artists have gone to the door and knocked, but I'm betting the black artists won't let 'em in.

Black heaven was where I tried to take my listeners through rhythm and verse. I turned them on to the poets of the Harlem Renaissance, finding messages that fit my groove. I would start injecting poetry around 7:45 in the morning—something unheard of on morning shows, which were supposed to be pure energy. A listener would call in on the air, and I'd read a snatch of my own inspiration: "I'm low this morning. Soothe me, darling. Life is over death, and love can never lose. I can hear your moans and promise you before this morning's out I'll mend your soul." Then I'd add this from Countee Cullen, written in 1925: "There is no stronger thing than song, in sun and rain, and leafy trees. It wafts the timid song along on crested waves of melodies." Wouldn't tell 'em where that came from till later, just segue right into "Only You."

Sometimes I'd end the show with my own verse: "O Negro slaves, dark, purple, ripened plums, / squeezed and bursting in the pinewood air, passing before they strip the old tree bare. / One plum was saved for me, one seed becomes an everlasting song, / a singing tree caroling softly souls of slavery. / My treasure of love is your history."

Then boom: "Treasure of Love," Clyde McPhatter.

I had to be different. I had to stand out. I had stumbled into a cauldron of history that had been withheld from me, and I was determined to use it on the air—not to preach, not to convert anybody, but to dazzle them, as I had been dazzled by the way the literature and the history of my people fit so perfectly with our popular music, the way that all forms of Negro communication are rooted in identical experience. It was a perfect fit. Mister Dunbar and Mister Reed had taught me that. Chicago had taught me that. But Chicago was not giving me enough to support my family. Rose had gone back to her mother's home in Lafayette to give birth to our son, Martin, and it seemed ridiculous to be struggling for a couple hundred dollars a week while the white deejay I was whipping, Howard Miller, was a millionaire. By the beginning of '57 something better came along. A Negro-oriented station in San Francisco wanted me as program director. I'd already spent practically a year and a half in the same job, far more than I'd ever spent at anything in my life. If you were going to chart my movements on a map, you were going to need a lot of sticking pins.

5 The Movement

Okay, if I'm the program director of a radio station in San Francisco, what am I doing on a plane to Boston? What am I doing in a car headed from Boston to Rhode Island? Why, I'm traveling to a conference that nobody has invited me to. I'm going to crash it and confront the governor of Arkansas about segregation. What else would an R&B deejay from San Francisco be doing?

But in September 1957 this all made perfect sense—poetic sense, at least. I told you when we began this journey that Negro deejays (the ones who could run their mouths like me, anyway) held a disproportionate social standing because black folk were shut out of virtually all white institutions. Who spoke for black people? Churches, certainly, on occasion. We'd been seeing that for nearly two years now, ever since Rosa Parks refused to give up her seat at the back of that bus in

Montgomery, sparking a bus boycott that became the first shot of the modern civil rights movement.

But churches could only take you so far. Churches could be bold but not audacious or politically down-and-dirty, and there were times when the evil of segregation loomed so grotesquely in the late fifties that grand gestures were demanded, and people like me became politicians without portfolios or planning, whether we'd ever registered to vote or not. (When I was working in Chicago, Al Benson had hired a plane before the presidential election in order to drop five thousand copies of the U.S. Constitution over his hometown of Jackson, "to wake up the citizens of Mississippi.")

Orval Faubus, the Arkansas governor, put me on that plane from San Francisco. Faubus was a Democrat whose election had been hailed by liberals, but a few days earlier he'd confounded the nation by blocking the federal-court-ordered integration of Central High in Little Rock. Nine black children, the first step toward total school desegregation in Little Rock, were turned away. Mobs of whites cursed and spat at the kids. It was ugly and shocking, and coming three years after the Supreme Court's ruling against segregated schools, it galvanized the national Negro community the way Rosa Parks's insult had galvanized Montgomery.

My station, KSAN, was broadcasting out of one of America's most liberal cities. The owner, the Reverend Norwood Patterson, was a white man with a conscience and an eye for the dramatic. I was doing three shifts a day on the station (6 to 8 A.M., 2:30 to 3:30 P.M., and 11 P.M. to midnight), but Patterson put himself, a couple of local businessmen, and me on a plane, aware that highly publicized meetings between Governor Faubus and President Eisenhower were supposed to be taking place that weekend in Newport.

Ostensibly we were going to deliver to the president the 4,000 telegrams, letters, and petitions that the station had collected from the people of the Bay Area in the days after the Little Rock Nine were turned away, begging for an end to racial violence in the South. At the same time, Patterson organized a rally in San Francisco for the following Sunday that was to feature one of the Little

Rock Nine, Elizabeth Eckford, and a minister, the Reverend M. L. Shuttlesworth, who'd been beaten by a white mob during a demonstration in Birmingham.

Then it became known that Faubus was going to hold a press conference in Providence. It was too irresistible a scene. So while some of the KSAN party stayed in Newport for an audience with Eisenhower's press secretary to turn over the telegrams, the rest of us drove to Providence, where a tense Faubus faced the public, simply reading a prepared statement defending his resistance of federal integration efforts.

I'm sure it will surprise you to know that I stood up and began shouting at him in front of the assembled reporters in a packed room.

I told him that little Elizabeth and Shuttlesworth were going to appear at the San Francisco rally the next day.

"That little girl says she's scared, but she wants to go back to school!" I cried. "Why don't you give the kids a chance to learn? Let them go back to school Monday, and if there's any trouble, then call out the national guard to protect them and not keep them out! White children and Negro children will make it if the adults will simply get out of their way and let them!"

The governor looked back at me grimly. "I did not come here to debate the question," he said and started pushing his way out of the room.

I'm sure it will surprise you that I cornered him at the door.

He looked at me as though I'd hurt his feelings, the way some white people did whenever Negroes were uppity enough to stand up for themselves.

"Why do you try to crucify me?" he asked. "I'm the most liberal governor in the South!"

"Do you call pointing guns at children 'liberal'?" I shouted, and we parted company, neither of us the wiser. I went back to the West Coast and held the rally; Faubus went back to Arkansas and, as was inevitable, gave up: a week later Elizabeth and the other eight children began attending classes.

I lasted less than a year in San Francisco. Los Angeles was too big and too close to resist. I'd passed through first as a runaway and then for a few weeks on that little station in Long Beach in '52, but this was different. Now I was somebody. Now I could own my biggest city yet.

It didn't happen the way I planned. I brokered my way into a midnight-to-4 A.M. shift, broadcasting on KGFJ, the city's black-oriented music station, from a picture-window studio in a record shop at Western and Vernon called Dolphins of Hollywood. It sounds like crap hours, but it was a powerhouse time slot in the eyes of independent record companies. They knew the deejay could play anything he wanted at these moments, anything that caught his fancy, any way he wanted. Every little singing group in L.A. knew it, too, so every night there'd be a knot of 'em, making pilgrimages with demos in hand or wanting to come inside and just perform. Record companies would hand carry the records that daytime deejays had branded "dogs" in the hope of getting a new ear. No matter what time, you always had company, on the air and outside your window.

There were a lot of surprises at those hours. My favorite happened before I was permanently based in L.A. It was September '57, the month of that political confrontation in Rhode Island. I had been flying down from San Francisco occasionally to broadcast from the Dolphins record shop, and on this night I had something special in my hands: the first pop song Sam Cooke had recorded, crossing over from gospel. Earlier in the year Sam's gospel group, the Soul Stirrers, had been in L.A. when somebody approached him at the Shrine Auditorium about trying his hand at a ballad. He could tell the time was right to combine his spirituality with the pop form. What came out of that session at Specialty Records under the hand of a producer named Bumps Blackwell had so much of that feeling, I couldn't contain myself when I heard it. On the air from Dolphins, I played the record and played it again. And again. I whispered on the microphone: "My darlings, does *your* darling send you? If your darling sends you, come to the record shop." And I played it again, savoring Sam's sweet voice, which sounded as if he were praising God yet looking into the eyes of his woman, telling her: "Darling, you send me—honest, you do." I played it again, ever more urging my darlings to come down to Dolphins. Outside the line of fans grew and grew, and damned if around 4 in the morning, Sam himself didn't come to the shop, climb into the booth, and sing "You Send Me," which would eventually rise to the nation's number-one pop song and sell 1.7 million copies. We kept it going until dawn.

I geared my show not merely to women, but to the dark, pure, black, ebony, brown-skin-in-heart-and-soul Negro women, not like the women you saw on Negro magazines that didn't want to put a dark woman on the cover, that served the "blue-vein society." (The first time I heard that phrase I was in Chicago, and somebody had to explain what it meant: Negroes whose skin was light enough to see the color of their veins.) I knew that the key to our struggle (and my audience) was the black woman, singing her soul out, singing of unity. She kept the family together, and many days I would take pains to fashion a black-woman mix: Dinah Washington, Nina Simone, Della Reese. I'd preface it by talking a little bit ("She's gonna explain the world and change the world"), and even if I didn't mention color, the sisters got the point, and the switchboard would light up and the calls would flood in: "But Montague, *I'm* light, I went to Fisk, but I'm not like that." "Montague, I am *indeed* a sister—I'm light, but I'm black in my heart all the way. Don't bring no more tears to my eyes." This was deep, and as they talked I would turn a background gospel track on, and I would say: "I'm going to recite a poem of mine to all of you, 'A Black Woman Speaks'":

> *It's true, my pearls were beads of sweat, wrung from weary bodies*
> *   pained.*
> *Instead of rings upon my hands, I wore swollen bursting veins.*
> *My ornaments were the whip-lashed scars, my diamond perhaps a*
> *   tear.*
> *Instead of paint and powder on my face I wore a solid mask of fear to*
> *   see my blood so spilled.*

And you, white women, spoke no protest,
but cuddled down in your pink slavery and thought somehow my
  wasted blood confirmed your superiority.
But we're going to move on up a little higher. And Mahalia Jackson is
  taking us on home.

And then, Mahalia, who would soon be singing at Doctor King's rallies, would come in with an oldie, the first million-seller in gospel history, "I Will Move on up a Little Higher." And that was why it didn't matter what goddamn hour of the day or night I was on. You give people a picture in their minds, and they will follow you anywhere.

The other jockeys in Los Angeles hated me, just like the jockeys in Chicago hated me, and there was nothing about it but jealousy (can you believe they considered me an arrogant SOB?). I didn't give a damn. Hell, L.A. was so barren, so segregated, that the most popular black deejay was a white man named Hunter Hancock. I'd be leaving soon.

Only three things happened this time around in L.A. that were truly meaningful. First, I spent several hours one day in a Long Beach secondhand shop, and as I was walking out, I saw a box by the door. What's in it? I asked the owner. Magazines damaged by mildew, he said. But something told me to look. And also lying in that box, in gold trim, was a 1906 biography of Frederick Douglass by Booker T. Washington. Mint condition. Mine. I still get goose bumps remembering that find.

Second, I made a lifelong friend of a tall L.A. cop who had a little singing group on the side, and of course he had that universal dream of laying down his badge and picking up that microphone full time. He found me and put a sample reel of tape in my hand. I listened and told him and his boys not to quit their day jobs. Might have done him a favor. If Tom Bradley had quit being a cop, he wouldn't have been elected to the city council, and he wouldn't have been mayor—both notions that would have sounded ridiculous to me there in '58, since there'd never been a Negro elected to the L.A. council. Of course, had I given Tom a helping hand in the music business, I also wouldn't have gotten fired for endorsing him for mayor on the air, but I'm getting way ahead of myself.

The third thing, which happened after I left KGFJ, was the last thing you'd expect from a boy who was practically expelled from his mother's church. It came to me that I should narrate a recording of portions of the Bible. For no apparent reason, pictures from the Old Testament appeared before me, as well as pictures from the Revelation of St. John the Divine.

Although scores of white actors had recorded parts of the Scriptures for major record companies' spoken-word divisions, up to that time I had never seen or heard of a Negro recording. I would be the first to do it for the mass market, through my own production company, but without the support of popular radio play, since I wasn't on the air.

I had never read more than two or three chapters of Revelation in my youth, but I did remember clearly the little storefront Church of God on First Street in Elizabeth and Elder McIvory preaching with wild fury his interpretation of the prophecies of the overthrow of Jerusalem. I'd been caught up in his drama, despite my determined uninterest, and I guess it had been lodged in my mind ever since. I fear the revelations with awesome vigor, more so than the other stories and miracles in the Bible, but I was intrigued and believed I could paint a picture. So I called my mother, not sure whether she'd laugh or cry, and told her what I was going to do. As she always said, because I had a hard head: "I'm praying for you," and "It's in you, so do it."

So I began to read, day and night. The book of Revelation consists of seven visions: the vision of the throne of God and the lamb, the vision of the seven seals, the vision of the seven trumpets, the vision of the woman and her enemies, the vision of the lamb and the angels of judgment, the vision of the seven vials, and the vision of the final triumph. Revelation ends as it begins, with the certainty that Christ is coming and that he will triumph over his enemies: Satan, sin, and death.

It was time to go into the studio. I had laid out for the engineers what sound effects were needed. By then it was as if I was in a daze. I knew I needed the sounds of wind, rain, thunder, and humans in agony, as well as echo. I read directly from the Bible. After three hours I was finished. We mixed in the sound effects and I went home, drenched in sweat, on cloud nine, and fell asleep.

I pressed 25,000 double LPs with a biblical cover reading "The Biblical Revelation of Saint John the Divine." It was considered a hit in the spoken-word category, but what mattered more was feeling, unaccountably, that the Lord was with me, that I was on a spiritual journey.

It was a journey that took me, after drifting through a couple of jobs I can barely remember (Colorado, a country-and-western station; Florida, where I got fired for failing to address the manager by his proper title), to St. Louis in 1960. It was trips like these, through the middle of the country where a black face was so rare, that an interracial couple, especially one with a young child, drew exceedingly strange looks. We were in a restaurant in Wyoming and a kid came over to the table and asked me why I hadn't washed my face. He'd never seen a Negro! Where would he? We were invisible. Another time in Iowa we checked into a motel late at night, got up early the next morning, and were pulling out onto the highway when I remembered I'd left my watch on the nightstand. By the time I went back in to get it and came out, the motel's manager and his wife were standing outside at the driveway, and when we drove back out again and they saw me (for the first time, since Rose, as always, had rented the room), the manager's mouth went wide open in shock, and so did his wife's. Nobody ever tried to run us out of town, but those looks . . . you remember.

KXLW was the station I landed on in St. Louis, but what I remember more than the music was a rabbi named Julius Nadel, who helped me bring to fruition a fascination with Judaism, a pull so strong that I literally became a Jew.

You could not be a Negro in the record business and not be curious about how these two tribes had mingled together in rhythm and blues. You would have to have been an idiot, first off, not to notice the number of Jews who ran independent companies specializing in black music: Art Rupe, founder of Specialty Records in L.A.; the Chess brothers, Phil and Leonard, in Chicago; Syd Nathan, who owned King records in Cincinnati; the Mesner brothers in L.A. with Aladdin Records, and Jerry Wexler, one of the hearts of Atlantic Records. You'd have to have been only a little less blind to ignore the fact that Jews, like blacks, had gravitated to the music business because there were so many covenants locking them out of more respectable professions. I knew that just about the only white people who'd ever given me a break in this business were Jews, and a fair number of times they did it not only because they knew I could make them some money but because they recognized my talent and genuinely wanted to help—genuinely identified with being on the wrong side of society's line. If you had ever considered the Old Testament, you would instinctively understand what Paul Robeson explained in a 1927 issue of the *Jewish Tribune:* "The Bible was the only form of literature the captive Negroes could get at, even those who could read. It was natural for their quick imaginations to find a . . . similarity between their condition and that of the enslaved Hebrews." Listen to the black voices sing: "Go down, Moses, way down in Egypt land; tell old Pharaoh to let my people go!"

We knew; all of us knew. We knew, too, from dealing with Jewish merchants in black neighborhoods and from being ripped off by Jews in the record business, that there were as many sinners as saints in this marriage, yet still we recognized the kinship. Personally I took it deeper. The more I collected history, the more it pained me that Negroes knew so little of their people's struggles and remarkable successes. By contrast, I realized, the Jews had managed to educate so many generations of their own. I thought, vaguely, that if I studied the Jews, I could learn something important. What kept them going in the face of so much hatred? How did they survive?

I met Rabbi Nadel because of where my family and I were living in St. Louis: right on the border between blackville and a Jewish neighborhood. I could see Nadel's synagogue from my window, and one day some unseen hand touched me on the shoulder and I walked over. Everybody looked at me, wondered what I was doing there. The rabbi came over and shook my hand, and we went into his office and hit it off. He, it turned out, was interested in blacks.

It was a hard time to reach out. St. Louis was still intensely segregated. I'll tell you a story that happened around the same time: Bobby Darin, the Atlantic Records artist, was just breaking big. He was a friend of mine. Bobby was the first white artist Atlantic had signed, and he loved black—black music, black people. He had some big shows booked in downtown St. Louis, and they set up a special night for a black audience. KXLW was a white-owned, black-oriented station, so the promoters gave us passes for colored night and said they would introduce us all from the stage, and all the black jocks said they'd be there that night. All except me. It was bad enough having to live in a city that still had segregated hotels and water fountains and restrooms; if the goddamn record company wanted me to play Bobby's records, they could let me come on the night I wanted.

Bobby doesn't know anything about this when he calls me at the station: "What's happening, baby?" I tell him I'm not coming. "Fuck it, then I'm not coming either, 'cause you my man!" he says. He calls Atlantic's founder, Ahmet Ertegun, to complain, and Ahmet (a Turk who I believe could pass for black) comes to St. Louis to talk to the concert-hall owner, who won't integrate the shows. I'm not asking that, Ahmet tells him, just let the black jockeys come to the white show. Okay, the owner says, if they sit in an assigned section. Sorry, no good. By now Bobby wants Magnificent Montague to introduce him to the crowd. More bitching about how This Is Unheard Of, but finally they relent, and so there I am, onstage before a white audience, with all these cute little white girls in the front rows waiting for Bobby, and I take the mike and say, "I'm Magnificent Montague . . ." They swoon, and the manager of the hall is fuming. (Just to piss off the manager afterward, Bobby walks me backstage and thanks him, one arm around me. It wasn't always just the Jews who were our brothers.)

So we're talking, Rabbi Nadel and me, and finally I just come out with it, as though I'm joking: "Why don't you teach me how to be Jewish, and I'll teach you how to be black? We'll trade this off."

"I like it," he says. We agreed that I would come every evening and study, and for every evening I would give him an hour on the history of blacks. I was buying more and more books, so this came as a delightful challenge to distill my growing collection. In fact, after a while I began to suspect the rabbi was getting more from me than I was getting from him. For six, maybe eight weeks this went on. I learned the story of the Jews, the Diaspora, the holidays, the rituals, the foundation of ethical monotheism that paved the way for Christianity. And on Adar 14 in the Hebrew year 5720 (more commonly known as March 13, 1960) Rabbi Nadel issued me a certificate of conversion. We went to dinner and celebrated, and he asked me to sum up what I'd learned about Jews and blacks.

It was so personal I had trouble finding words. I'd found similarities in the spirituality both sides bring to the table, I told him, but Jews have an advantage I envied: each of their religious holidays represents something historically significant to their people. Imagine, as a parent, the power that gives you—the tools it gives you by presenting each holiday to your child as a lesson in how to live his life, a lesson tied directly to real life, a way to reinforce values so the old mistakes or injustices will not occur again. That is what bands the Jews together, that and their intense pride in achievement.

"Rabbi," I said, "the only thing that bands my people together is our religious fervor, but we don't have a racial religion, or holidays significant enough to loop it in right with our religion, with our hand clapping. We do have one thing that no one else has, though. We have the Gift, the gift of song, the touch that song has given Negroes. God gave the Semitic people certain gifts, and in the same regard he gave us music." Music had been so wrapped up in so many phases of my life, I took it for granted. It was as common as the air, and just as essential to my people's survival. Maybe it was the passage of time that was making me more introspective. I was thirty-two, and moving city to city was taking its toll. The next market I wanted was the biggest, and the one that was next door to home.

6 The Apple

"Boy, don't you do that!"

Do what? I was taking a *piss!*

As a collector, one of the things I loved about being on the air in New York in 1962 was its proximity to so many other eastern cities and the density of old materials awaiting my hunting eye.

Today I was going to search for more of them, driving down to Washington to an out-of-the-way bookstore an old collector had told me about, a hole-in-the-wall place with some juicy finds. I had almost gotten there when nature called, badly. I passed the D.C. train station and, yes, I knew there was segregation in D.C., but I didn't apply it to the station. I hightailed it inside the men's room and was about to let the rhythm flow when I heard that booming, accusatory voice from behind. Don't *do* that? I couldn't hold it back. I was already into my first verse, and the sax wanted to blow, and the next thing I knew, a hand came upside my head.

I hit the ground. My pants were wet. They dragged me out and dumped me on the ground and said, "Boy, *that's* where you go." That's when I saw the "colored" sign, and I crawled in there and cleaned myself up. The colored restroom worker looked at me pitifully. "Can't you read?" he said.

"I didn't know I couldn't go to the restroom there."

"Where you from?"

"New York."

"Y'all up there, you got an attitude."

I asked him who the hell's side he was on and walked away, telling myself again and again not to get angry, just be on your mission, find some books. I found the bookstore, walked in, and looked into the face of an ol' redneck cracker behind the counter. "Boy, what you want?" He sounded hateful from the start.

If I didn't talk right to him, I'd never see any gems, and talking "right" to them was being able to con them when they thought they were misusing me. I knew he was an ignorant, hateful, y'all-come-back jive dealer. He wasn't accepted by the real rare-book shops 'cause he was running a schlock outfit—no class, chewing tobacco, wearing suspenders. But oh, he knew how to find gems, white or black, if you could stand his ignorance and pay his price.

"I'm looking for something about colored folks," I said.

"Well, boy, come over here to this table. I got some things about slavery and the Civil War, and I do business with the Smithsonian, and Harvard; I don't do business with that nigrah school up there [Howard University]. They too uppity. I got somethin' back here you ought to see. Come back here, boy."

What I saw made me want to jump.

It was the first issue of the first Negro magazine, published and printed in Philadelphia in 1898, mint condition, with a letter from the publisher to his daughter. It was called *Music Pictorial,* twelve pages, with the inscription "Written and Edited by Members of Our Race" and the motto "We Are Rising." I didn't know it existed, only that somewhere there was supposed to be a Negro magazine that predated all known ones. It's not listed in any of the reputable reference books because it was discontinued. Like ephemera, it had gotten lost.

I looked up, feigning uninterest. "You got anything else?" He showed me around a bit more, but there wasn't anything I cared about.

"Well, sir," I said, "I don't got much money but I think I'd like that old music magazine. How much would that cost me?"

He almost spat at me. "Boy, you think I'm a fool?"

"No, sir."

"I already got an inquiry from the Smithsonian. I know what it is, boy. It's something rare. I don't care nothing about it, but I know they want it. What you gonna do with it?"

"Well, you know, sir, I try to find items so I can help my people, and I'd appreciate it if you'd let me do that, 'cause I'm gonna show it around, and it's people like you, with these little shops, who are going to keep the history of colored folks alive." I said it very soft, said it directly into his eyes.

He said, "All right, gimme thirty-five hundred dollars.

I thought he was gonna say three hundred. You figure, roughly, a dollar or two for every year out of print. I had $750 in my pocket for my spending spree in Washington. I went back to the car and grabbed some traveler's checks. Then I realized it was seven at night and I wouldn't be able to cash them, so I found a phone and called a dealer in Greenwich Village who'd sold me a lot of stuff recently, a good friend. I told him about the dilemma.

"I'll talk to him," he said.

I wandered back inside the store. "Listen, all I got in cash is $650, but I've got a friend in New York—"

"That ain't gonna do you no good—"

"named Walter Goldwater."

That did it. "*You* know Walter Goldwater?"

They talked on the phone for maybe thirty seconds, and the cracker went into the back and came out with the magazine wrapped up. "Look," he said, "if you need that six-fifty for yourself right now, just take this, 'cause Goldwater guaranteed it."

Walter, whose University Place Bookshop specialized in Negro material, had told the cracker I was buying the book for him and demanded 20 percent off. I mailed the cracker a check for $2,800. Today that magazine is worth fifteen times that much. What determines price? Whatever the dealer can squeeze out of you, and I would have sucked his ass in Macy's window to get this one.

If I was back home, it was not exactly in Elizabeth, New Jersey, and not exactly in Manhattan, but close enough. I was in Woodside, Long Island, broadcasting on WWRL, "New York's all-Negro station," which you could hear clear out to the Virgin Islands. No time slot available but dog time when I got there—midnight till 3 A.M., find your own sponsors—but it didn't take me two weeks before I'd sold all that time, plus another three hours, so that I was broadcasting midnight till 6. It wasn't long, either, before I started hearing the high school principals complain, the same way I'd heard 'em complain in L.A., that too many of these kids were staying up too late just so they could dial me up and shout out a one-sentence dedication and make themselves part of the Montague Mix. Would I please *do* something? What? Tell 'em to drink a glass of warm milk? Finally the station came up with a compromise: it cut me back to three hours at night and added two hours a day in the afternoon.

But there was nothing they could do to diminish the power of what I was doing. It wasn't simply me; it was the intensity of the music and the intensity of the times. When you listen to R&B from 1962 and 1963, my years in the Big Apple, it's impossible to separate it from the power of the civil rights movement, the awakening of the Negro race, and the gospel influences that were driving everything. So that when I said "Wake *up,* New York!" or "Are you *ready* for it, New York?" or "Can I get a *witness*?" black folk heard it with a racial ear—not simply because of my implication, or because of the record I was playing, but because they were caught up in the most racially charged days of our lives, days when Negroes and their white allies routinely put their lives on the line to protest segregation, when the future was still up for grabs, when evil was still

in the ball game, when you had to be ready. Play Ray Charles or
Solomon Burke or Sam Cooke or Curtis Mayfield from those particular years—I swear they sound different, more soulful. They had
to be; they were living those times, too. More young men were following Sam Cooke's example and leaving spiritual music for the
pop side of the street, and when those boys and those times collided, a grand force swept over us, and we called it s-o-u-l music.

Take the summer of '63. There was a tremendous mobilization
for the March on Washington, which would be immortalized by
Martin Luther King Jr.'s "I Have A Dream" speech, and the line
between deejay and minister was easily blurred. I was shouting out
to my listeners that they needed to rise up and be counted, to put
on their walking shoes. "I ain't gonna let nothing turn me around!"
I'd say, and I'd drop Ray Charles on 'em. "Now is the time!" I'd say.
"We are tied together by oppression. Call me now and say you're
gonna walk that walk and talk that talk, and if the line is busy get
on that other line, get on that telephone to Heaven and call on the
Lord." It was nothing but pure theatrics, but it was also the forerunner of the electronic preacher. You were playing songs about
misery ("Drown in My Own Tears," as Ray Charles comes aboard)
and heartbreak ("Release Me," thank you, Little Esther Phillips),
but you were showcasing them with a desire to cleanse the soul, to
give your audience an experience that was not merely fun but ca-
thartic, wild, exhausting, so devoted to these values that it became
a spiritual act, a religion in itself. Plenty of white kids started to find
out about the secret world that lay at the far right end of the AM
dial, at 1600. There weren't any Beatles quite yet (fueled in part by
copying that soul) to feed that same kind of unfocused hunger.

The theme song I played every night to open my show was a
three-minute sermon titled "Montague the Magnificent." I
brought Cissy Houston (Whitney's mother), Dee Dee Warwick (Dionne's sister) and Aretha Franklin into the studio to chant my
name: "Montague . . . the magnificent . . . the man of soul . . . to
entertain you!" with a surging gospel organ underneath, and over
it all I welcomed my darlings lovingly and then began to shout
between deep breaths:

When the burdens of life get you down!
When all your friends seem to turn their backs on you!
When you walk along the street in the early morning!
When you're off to work!

Then I'd calm down and continue, soothingly:

I want you to think about me.
I want you to hold me close to your heart and call me
When you rise in the morning and all seems dark.

Then I'd take it up again:

When you feel there's nothing left in life,
I want you to reach—
PUT YOUR HAND ON YOUR RADIO! TOUCH MY HEART!
Burn my heart with desire!

And then I would give a long scream and, sounding almost sexually excited, continue.

Now, darling, hum the song with me . . . hum it, darling
[Here the singers would hum a background melody.]
I've found my heart
And your love.

As I spoke my last line, the singers faded out on their last moan, and the organ put itself to bed as well. And *then* you were ready for my show to start.

I had a particularly close relationship with Atlantic Records as a consultant—hell, I had an office inside their building on Broadway—and in deference to me they put the theme song out as a single, only to be amazed when it sold 200,000 copies in New York.

I was where I had dreamed about being, feeding off all this emotion, this energy, this volatility, reveling in the unintended consequences of my audacity. The great singer Lloyd Price, who'd become a friend, had his own record label now, and he had a new singer he was pitching and gave me a dub, so I threw it in my briefcase and said I'd listen. That night, must have been pure accident, I threw it in a stack of records I would play on the air. I worked in a darkened studio, for the mysticism and the sense of performance, so at one point I played the dub and out came: "If you neeeed me, calllll me . . ." The voice, which turned out to be Wilson Pickett's, inflamed me, so after a couple stanzas, I shouted over it: "I know tonight *someone* out there needs me to help them find the way to love. Say it again, son!" And I backed "If You Need Me" up to that line again. This is what it felt like for a record to *burn,* and somewhere during my tenure in New York I started to shout it when I got moved: "Burn, baby! Burn!" Nothing calculated, just another collision between emotion and alliteration. Don't remember how or when it came to me, just that the good ideas seemed to stick.

Now, Pickett was nobody back then, another gospel shouter trying to cross over, but you could hear him for the first time in your life and know he had the kind of voice that brought out in listeners what a great preacher brings out in his congregation—he brought alive the amen corner, those people you see who are high on spirit, alive with emotion, joyously dancing, taking the service to a higher level, responding to the preacher as he speaks. "What shall it profit a man to gain the world and lose his soul?" the preacher might ask, and Sister Joan's or Brother William's voice shoots out like punctuation, not melodically but plaintively: "I don't *need* no money." "My soul's *gone* to glory." "This ol' world *ain't* my home." Wilson Pickett had that skill that separated an average preacher from a superstar preacher.

I kept cueing the same line from the song over and over: "If you neeeeed me, calllll me." I started acting as Pickett's amen corner, singing my own parenthetical lines between his:

If you need me
(Have mercy!)
Call me
(Call Montague, darling!)
If things go wrong

(I'm here to soothe your soul!)
I'll be home . . .

"I need phone calls only from the brokenhearted!" I said, and the calls began:

"I need Henry . . ."

"I need Doris . . ."

"I need Dolores . . ."

It went on for an hour, until about 1:30 in the morning. By 2:00 people were down at the station asking where they could get a copy of the record. Lloyd Price called, happy but frantic: "Montague, we got a hit on our hands but we ain't *got* no records!" He hadn't pressed anything but the dub yet.

I began to understand that, in their own way, these artists, even the most anonymous, were leaders, simply because of the way they fed the audience's bodies with dance, their hearts with melody, their heads with the belief that they could make it through the pain. The Negro elite would never glorify these performers; they came from across the tracks, unschooled, unsophisticated, making a living this way because all the other doors were shut, no dreams beyond the day, beyond putting bread on the table. Yet what they gave to the people, and to themselves, was profound: song and dance to quench the thirst, to stop the hunger, to make 'em laugh in spite of having no chance, none to none. They used rhythm and rhyme to construct a bridge that still stands, and on that bridge the traffic is still overflowing, the bridge of music, the bridge of song that got black souls over and that crossed over into the American popular culture.

I had to use that bridge creatively if I was going to keep paying $2,800 every time I got excited about a piece of history. I had to do something nobody else was doing. When you think New York and Negroes you think the Apollo in Harlem, but deejays did nothing but emcee those shows. I wanted a piece of it. So at the end of '62 I paid $1,500 to use a big auditorium called Rockland Palace at 155th and 8th Avenue in the Bronx on the edge of Harlem. I went to Vee

Jay and those other black independent labels and said: "Gimme dubs on any artist you got coming out that's within 300 miles of this area, and I'll bust them records. All you got to give me in exchange is those artists for my show." They started to add up: Jimmy Reed, John Lee Hooker, Dionne Warwick, Don and Dewey, Sam and Dave, Gene Chandler, Ben E. King—a lot of those people were just on the margins in '62, or else they had only regional reputation—and I got more, too: Rufus Thomas, the Shirelles, Little Esther. Then I cut a deal with the record shops: they'd sell my tickets ($2.50) in exchange for a few hundred in free goods of my concert artists, which we'd split the profits on—and we knew those records would get hot 'cause Montague was gonna be getting down on those dubs on the air.

We threw one more artist on as an afterthought. He was the twenty-fourth performer listed of twenty-five on the poster. Stax Records in Memphis had been recording a band called the Pine-toppers. They had a half-hour left over in the studio and decided to waste it on a solo by somebody in the group. They took the cut to a white R&B deejay in Nashville, John Richbourg, who says, "Okay, I'll play it, but give me half the publishing," and he gets a few phone calls from listeners. Stax starts plugging it, calls me in New York, and I tell them I'll play it only if they give me this singer for my Rockland show *and* the Stax act I really want, Booker T. and the MGs. And that's how Otis Redding made his first trip to New York—hell, his first road trip!—to sing "These Arms of Mine." (You want to know what kind of a budget these singers performed on? Once Otis was playing the Howard Theater in Washington, two shows a day, and early in one of his sets he throws his hat, Frisbee-style, into the audience, which freaks. A song later he throws his sunglasses, then his sports jacket, then his handkerchief, shoes, socks, tie, vest, shirt, undershirt . . . and then, at the end of the set, the theater makes somebody come out of the orchestra pit and plead for the clothes back, offering to pay five dollars an article, since Otis didn't have but one set of clothes for the whole week of shows. A fan remembers watching a girl clutching the hat, being dragged away by two ushers, screaming, "I'll die before anyone gets this outta me!")

I called my concert "Montague's Down Home Soul Show and Dance," since so much of my radio show was down in the bucket, and started promoting it on the air a month ahead of time. I needed a gimmick, so I decided to use a new John Lee Hooker song, "Send Me Your Pillow." First off, I declared that the first part of my radio show was for women only. If you're a man, don't even listen. Don't you *dare* listen, you unfaithful dogs. Women, you call me with your problems. I'll take care of them. And most of all, darlings, send me your pillow. Thousands of them began to come in to the studio (with, of course, a few accompanying threats on my life from boyfriends; I had to get a couple of bodyguards for a while).

A few days before the show, Sam Cooke, who was in New York getting ready to tour, told me he wanted to have lunch to talk about me producing a recording by L. C., his brother, because Sam was too close to him. Sam saw one of the posters I was carrying, saw the lineup, and started laughing. "Montague, what is this? You got everybody and their mother in this show!"

The night the concert rolled around, to my surprise, I had Sam, too.

It was past two in the morning when he walked in. The show was still going strong, ten thousand people, and when I say people I mean family, all generations, not like today, when all you get is the youngsters. By the financial grace of Jerry Wexler at Atlantic, Booker T. and the MGs were backing each act; I hadn't been able to book a backing act. I'd limited each artist to one song, but black artists won't quit, and we weren't close to being finished. Backstage Sam was being mobbed by the other performers. That type of camaraderie was rare; there's a lot of jealousy among black artists, but Sam was like the Messiah. He went dressing room to dressing room, talking to 'em, having a ball, singing with them. I was out on stage, and at one point, when I said, "Can I get a witness?" Sam stepped out on stage, took the microphone, and said, "*I'm* your witness, Montague," and the ladies went mad, waving their pillows and their hankies. He opened up with, of all things, a spiritual hit, "Touch the Hem of His Garment," whose first soaring syllables alone ("There was a woman . . .") were an entire church service, and as he sang the auditorium fell silent. And then the other artists came out and began to join Sam in the song. It would be my last show with him.

I was reading a lot now from my mushrooming collection, six or seven books or magazines at a time, lost in the eighteenth and nineteenth centuries, dazed by a feeling of being transported through time, trying to form a picture in my mind: How did this happen to us? How did we get to this place? There was no shortage of authoritative voices on the street ready to answer these questions. The sharpest of them, on the prowl in Harlem, was Malcolm X, preaching the separatist doctrine of the Nation of Islam: "Beware of the blue-eyed devil! The devil's in Harlem and he's got blond hair and blue eyes! He's your enemy and he's mine." He soared above all the rhythmic patterns and philosophies—the best Negro preachers could not touch this voice. Malcolm X came with the sensibilities of an antebellum preacher and the razor-cut articulation of a Wall Street lawyer. Shouts of accompaniment greeted his pronouncements. He was takin' em down to de mire, down to the dirt, bending their knees with make-sense song. "Make it plain, Brother Malcolm!" they would urge him again and again, and he would, and you did not have to agree with the answer to admire the mathematical intellect that went into his historical calculations.

The owner of a big bookshop at 125th Street in Harlem introduced me to Malcolm, and while we didn't have much in common beyond the fact that we were both making a living with our voices and street wits, he was intrigued by my history collection. He never tried to recruit me, never said, "I need you to join the Muslims." Remember, I went clear back to Boston with Louis Farrakhan, who was by then among Malcolm's chief rivals in a power struggle inside the Nation of Islam—a struggle growing out of Malcolm's shock at news that his former mentor, the Honorable Elijah Muhammad, had impregnated several women.

On some nights Malcolm spent hours in my apartment comb-
ing through my collection. Stored inside his computer-like mind
(he had, after all, taught himself to read in prison by reading the
dictionary, word by word, front to back) were hundreds of sayings
and revolutionary verses written by unknown authors and poets.
His ability to assimilate knowledge and instantly place it in his
political context and speak it so lyrically astonished me. One of his
favorite quotes was from the Russian poet Aleksandr Pushkin, who
was descended on his mother's side from Abraham Petrovich
Hannibal, an African slave who became a favorite of Czar Peter I.
"Oh, shake and shiver tyrants of the world," Pushkin wrote. "But
lend an ear, ye fallen slaves, gain courage and arise."

I was one of the few allowed to breech Malcolm's wall of security at his Nation of Islam rallies, placing my small reel-to-reel tape
recorder near him, setting my microphone next to his, testing it
by saying "Can I get a witness?" and hearing the crowd thunder:
"Have mercy, Montague." And while the last year of Malcolm's
life, 1964, would be devoted to a less fierce, more reasoned inter-
national view of race, his true force was on display in those earlier
speeches at what he called "unity rallies," many hours of which I
have retained in my collection. Listen to this from a chilly afternoon:

> So in calling this unity rally, we invited Dr. Adam Clayton
> Powell, Dr. Roy Wilkins, Dr. Whitney Young, Dr. James Farmer,
> the Right Reverend Dr. Martin Luther King, Dr. Ralph Bunche,
> Dr. A. Philip Randolph. We invited all these doctors to come
> out and give their analysis, their diagnosis, of the ailments that
> our people are afflicted with here in America. We told them if
> they came out they would give you and us here in Harlem some
> idea what we can do to solve our problems instead of always
> running downtown to the white man to tell him what's wrong
> and begging him for crumbs. Our condition has to be corrected
> ourselves. No white man can do it for us. No white man will do
> it for us. No white man *wants* to do it for us. No white man even
> has the *nature* to do it for us.

The applause is deafening, even though most of the people in the crowd are Baptists and Methodists, people simply yearning for answers, for a message stronger than their own preachers were giving them. Above their approval, Malcolm continues: "You have to excuse me for being blunt speaking and frank talking. Mr. X speaks his mind. He tells the truth, whether you like it or not. He tells you the truth whether the white man likes it or not. We don't *care* who likes it or not, as long as we know it's the truth."

Who followed Malcolm? Very few. The Muslims have never had more than 20,000 members at most. Malcolm X never became a historical figure because the blacks in the church, the blacks who locked hands with the so-called Christian whites during the civil rights movement, were turned off by him. They were the ones saying, "Hey, leave X alone. He's dangerous; he's talking shit. He's talking about going back to Africa. He's talking this blue-eyed-white-man stuff." Spike Lee tried to make Malcolm a historical figure in his biopic but he failed because Spike doesn't understand black history. Once you heard Malcolm talk, you heard all he had to say! His life itself had no more than that: Boom—he's a pimp. Boom—he's in prison. Boom—he joins the Muslims. That big crowd scene in Mecca Spike did with people praying don't mean a damn thing to the American Negro, 'cause he ain't into that turn-east stuff. Malcolm was not a Gandhi. Gandhi was about humility. This man was about kickin' ass. The movie was cerebral. In truth, Malcolm was about an eye for an eye, and that's why I kept all those tapes. They show what Malcolm was, in the best sense: not a leader—he had no organized group—but an articulate, dynamic race speaker. A race speaker as Frederick Douglass was a race speaker. A race speaker, telling it like it was, like W. E. B. Du Bois, the most influential black intellectual of his day, was a race speaker. Defining rather than leading. ("One feels," Du Bois said, "his two-ness—an American, a Negro, two souls, two thoughts, two un-reconciled strivings, two warring ideals in one dark body.") Blacks were already being led. It was King and all the other church leaders who got the people out. Malcolm X was more dangerous than any of them not because of what he advocated but because his intelligence was greater, great enough to draw a straight line between history and today, great enough to explain the universe to us, great enough to offer an answer to the question of how we got into this mess.

I kept dabbling with history on the air. I was always hollering "Can I get a witness?" but one night I told 'em that for the next hour the "can I get a witness" phone line would be limited to people with questions or observations about Negro achievements —they had thirty seconds to make a dedication, request a song, and make a short and soulful statement about black history. "What was our first record company?" somebody wanted to know. That would be Black Swan, which became very competitive with white companies in the twenties, I said. They signed up Ethel Waters ("Down Home Blues"), Alberta Hunter ("Bring Back the Joys"), Eubie Blake ("Sweet Georgia Brown"), plenty more. I didn't talk about why Black Swan died. That was going to come soon, in a different setting, with profound stakes.

I'd known Berry Gordy since he'd founded Motown. Every black jockey had. The jockeys were the only reason Gordy had survived. Like all small labels, Motown was at the mercy of white distribution systems. You didn't know how long it would take, once you shipped the records to a wholesaler and then to a distributor, to get the check back from the distributor. To a company with no cash flow, that could prove a disaster. The white-owned companies had more black artists than the black-owned companies had, more established influence with radio stations and better promotional staffs; the black-owned companies were struggling just to put the damn product out. So no matter what city I was working in, I felt an allegiance to the black-owned companies—Motown, Vee Jay, and Duke/Peacock in particular; if they told me they were getting slow pay from a distributor, I might call the distributor and say cut that check pronto, or I'm cutting off airplay for the other labels you distribute—and they knew I'd do it, because my mix relied on my yelling and raving as much as the hits of the day to make it work.

Gordy had the ear, an awesome ear, no question, but he recog-

nized that the business side of Motown had not developed the so-
phistication of the creative side. He'd left that part to his sister, and
she was learning the hard way that you couldn't press a half-mil-
lion copies of the next Miracles single if your accounts receivable
were in the toilet. And he also worried, in this most racially con-
scious of eras, that he had made a political mistake by packing his
business side—distribution, promotion, marketing—with white
executives. He was hearing a lot about that, and much of the flak
was coming from black deejays.

It wasn't unusual for record companies to retain deejays as consultants—it was an easy way to put money in our pockets, for one
thing—but now Gordy was asking me to do something different:
fly down to Detroit and basically do a day-long seminar for his
entire staff on how to buck up the business side. He seemed to have
run out of answers.

"Montague, I've hired these white people—it doesn't matter,
it's business."

"I agree, but you got to put some blacks in training quick. But
you can't train 'em 'cause you don't know. You're good in the studio. That's what you do. But you are going to lose out if you don't
control this question: is Motown basically, underneath, white-
controlled?"

The day I came down, they closed Motown at noon, served a
buffet lunch, and we started. I tried to do it like a show, right down
to beginning with "Can I get a witness?" I talked historically, about
black participation in American popular music, the famous songs
that nobody ever had a clue blacks wrote. (Not long before that I'd
purchased one of the two existing original copies of an 1855 composition by Richard Milburn, a Negro barber from Philadelphia
who was a marvelous whistler and guitar player, called "Listen to
the Mockingbird"—one of only two tunes to sell more than 20
million sheet music copies. The publisher took Milburn's name off
and gave credit to a white composer; my copy includes both
Milburn's name and his soon-altered original title: "Listen to the
Mockingbird: an Ethiopian Melody"—*Ethiopian* was just another
phrase of the day, another way they sectionalized and margin-

alized colored people rather than calling us Negroes, because they knew that would have given us too much power.) I talked about "cover" versions of black hits that whites used to steal our gifts. I took 'em through Negro spirituals, minstrels, blues, ragtime, syncopated jazz, race music . . . and I told them about the flourishing of Black Swan, decades before anybody thought of Motown—how Black Swan was squeezed out by the major record companies, how it wound up having to lease its recordings to the majors and ultimately faded away, leaving us in the situation we still faced and were trying to overcome: whites handling the product, and Negroes still just making the music.

Motown is not like that, I said, but there is a problem. When you have whites heading up your main sources of distribution and collecting the money, you must be careful, because most of them are thieves. They bear watching. You know the distribution agreements, you know the deals on the records, you know how to get the money under the table—and the best way to safeguard this is, I suggest, to have your white business people on top and put the blacks right there by their sides, and if there's going to be any thieving or stealing, let the blacks get a piece. You people are busy in the studio, on the road—everybody else must learn the record business. Berry wants you to learn the business.

Oh, I stood up there hip and confident that day, pouring out my heart, letting loose my acquired knowledge, and maybe I did some people some good. But a deeper question nagged at me. My history collection was beginning to confront me like a mounting, excessive gift from a genie. The more I bought, the more I sought. For years, like so many novice collectors, I had been consumed with the often-mindless chase, blessed with increased economic fortunes that allowed me to keep buying and blessed with the most tolerant of wives who shared my interest in history. Now, though, I was literally crowding myself out of our apartment. And I was increasingly consumed not merely by the chase but by the need to take stock of what I had been accumulating.

That's the only reason I can imagine why I invented a black ghetto boy named Henry J. and sent him out into the wilderness.

7 The Boy

Henry J. was born because of a trip I took upstate in New York sometime in 1963 looking for artifacts. I bought an old leather-bound Bible, and one night I was thumbing through it idly when I got the cock-eyed notion that the adventures I was collecting paralleled the Negro experience and that I should try to tell the historical journey the way the Bible told stories. It was the force of the times, of feeling pulled along. I thought that I would tell it through the eyes of a youngster. And I got my typewriter and my collection, and over the next several months I typed in my spare time until I had two hundred pages about the last visions of a dying teenage boy. No agent, no contract, no plans. Just typed pages.

"I learned early in life," Henry J. tells the reader, "to expect the pains of being black and to roll the best I could with the blows. I also learned that no matter how hard a white man tries to convince me of his sincerity, liberal ideas and ideologies, his faith in God and his sense of fair play, hidden underneath burned a growing complex of guilt and sorrow."

Henry continues:

> On this final twilight of my life, sick and dying, I knew that something was pushing me. I imagined many hidden and deep mystic visions, but on this night a voice seemed to be directly speaking to me:

> *When I consider how light is spent,*
> *Ere half my days in this dark world and wide,*
> *And that one talent which is death to hide*
> *Lodg'd with me useless, though my soul more bent*
> *To serve there with my maker, and present*
> *My true account. . . .*

This inner voice kept repeating the words "My true account, stand and wait, stand and wait." Perhaps I was crazy. . . .

I looked around but I could not see. I heard the voice within me speak again: "The issues, that's the question, equality, justice, materialistic realism." These things I could not understand. And again the voice spoke: "One day millions of black men will be free!" I tried to rise from my sickbed but I could not. Many voices spoke in unison.

I saw "TRUTH" written in a strange lettering of gold and blue, and in the middle of the clouds was a man dressed in garments of many different colors such as I had never seen before. Burning red and golden flames leaped all about him, but he did not speak. His eyes twinkled like stars, his mouth opened wide, and written words came rolling out, just as the waters roll on a stormy sea. And then, one by one, they appeared: the old and the young, not in the flesh as I, but in words shaped like a double-edged sword: Great men, leaders, ex-slaves, and under their man-word image there was a clear pool of tears and the sun beamed brightly about them. I stood, dazzled, afraid and ashamed of my fear. I wanted to ask questions but dared not.

I walked on until my eyes beheld the Master of the Book of Life. . . . He said, "I am what they on earth have written out of history. Look at me. . . . This is the Hall of Fame. . . . Come with me into the days of old and I will show you the truth of being black, and you shall see what black men accomplished that history soon forgot."

And the journey begins. The Master shows Henry black Hannibal of Carthage and tells him how Hannibal led twenty thousand men across the Alps and defeated the Roman army. He introduces him to Simon of Cyrene, his black brother who helped Christ carry the cross. Henry sees the great African Imhotep, who lived almost 3,000 years before Christ and was called the father of medicine. He learns how Tyro, an African secretary to Cicero, invented shorthand writing.

On through history the boy and the Master travel, seeing slavery established by Spain and Portugal, watching a Spanish Negro slave named Estevanico in one of the earliest expeditions through the New World. Then another voice speaks: "Hear me, lad. I am the voice of moral consciousness. I am full of sadness, and sorrow clings to my soul. Hear me, Henry J. There is an evil which I have seen under the sun and it is common among men who lack knowledge and wisdom. It is better to hear the rebuke of the wise than for a man to hear the songs of fools. Come let us learn to know, to search and to seek out wisdom, for wisdom strengthens knowledge."

Henry watches slavery extend its grip from one American colony to the next. He watches Crispus Attucks, an escaped slave, become possibly the first Negro to give his life for America in 1770. He reads the names of the Negro soldiers at Bunker Hill. He sees northern states abolish slavery, and he sees the price of a black man in the South rise from $500 in 1800 to $1,800 by the start of the Civil War.

As the Master takes him through the Hall of Fame, Henry meets Benjamin Banneker, the self-educated mathematician who made the first clock produced in America. He meets Phillis Wheatley, the slave girl who published her first book of poems in 1773, and George Bridgetower, the brilliant violinist whose performance of a Beethoven sonata once brought the composer to tears. He shakes hands with General Toussaint L'Ouverture, the ex-slave who boldly fought against the grand army of Napoleon to emancipate Haiti. He shivers in the presence of Frederick Douglass, the great Negro abolitionist and orator. He discovers James Hewlett, who in the 1820s, before the days of the minstrel shows, was playing Othello and Richard III in New York. His eyes fill with tears as he holds the hand of Harriet Tubman and learns of her underground railroad and the selflessness that won her the nickname "Moses" among the thousands of slaves she helped.

I made sure the boy was introduced to every facet of my collection, which now seemed to cover every inch of black history—years before there was a movement to create a formal field of study. I wanted to communicate Henry J.'s welling sense of astonishment and pride, the emotions I felt so often as I encountered new material. I made sure Henry met the people that I had told Motown's staff about that day in Detroit: W. C. Handy, the father of the blues, and Harry T. Burleigh, who studied under Antonin Dvořák and assisted him in his *New World Symphony.* I made sure he saw the dark hands of Dr. Daniel Hale Williams, the first American surgeon to operate successfully on the human heart in 1893, and Garrett A. Morgan, who invented the first American stoplight in 1922. I made sure he listened to a story that the Negro professor Booker T. Washington told at a cotton exhibition in Atlanta in 1895:

> A ship lost at sea for many days suddenly sighted a friendly vessel. From the mast of the unfortunate vessel was seen a signal: "Water, water, we die of thirst!" The answer from the friendly vessel at once came back: "Cast down your bucket where you are." A second time the signal—"Water, water, send us water!"—ran up from the distressed vessel, and was answered again: "Cast down your bucket where you are." The captain of the distressed vessel, at last heeding the injunction,

cast down his bucket, and it came up full of fresh sparkling water from the mouth of the Amazon River. To those of my race who depend upon bettering their condition in a foreign land, or who underestimate the importance of cultivating friendly relations with the Southern white, who is his next-door neighbor, I would say: "Cast down your bucket where you are"—cast it down in making friends in every manly way of the people of all races by whom we are surrounded.

Henry J. takes all this in, the story and the hundreds of people he has met in what appear to be four continuous days of travel that in fact take less than half an hour, and he asks the Master: "Sir, is this all true?"

"Yes, it is all true, but sit a spell, boy, and laugh injustice away."

We hear a comedian's voice: "They claim in certain parts of the South this is the coldest it's been in the Deep South in a hundred years. Now, I can't go along with that. Hell, I remember when I was a kid back home it got so cold one night the Ku Klux Klan tried to burn a cross on our front porch and we opened the door and told them, 'Bring it inside.' And they did. . . ."

"Henry J., here's the clincher." We hear a comedienne's voice:

Once upon a time, a tiny Negro girl lived in the Deep South. Every time she left her home, she had to sit in the back of the bus, the back of the streetcar, the back of the movie theater, the back of the church, the back of this and the back of that. But while she was still a little girl, her family moved to the far North. One day her mother took her to the most wonderful fairyland her eyes had ever seen. It was a beautiful amusement park with swings and slides and tunnels and boats and roller coasters and, best of all, a merry-go-round. The little child was simply entranced and fascinated by the merry-go-round, but she was afraid and puzzled, too. Finally as the music stopped and the merry-go-round slowed down, the girl turned to her mother and cried, "Oh, Mother, tell me please, where is the back of the merry-go-round?"

Now Henry J. applauds loudly, thanks Dick Gregory and Moms Mabley for their few moments of satire, and moves on.

The spirit leads Henry to the Congregation of the Ungodly, where he watches a slave owner be interrogated: "Did you not say slaves were 'devisable like other chattel, having no right to religion, to be sold no less than land, horse or ox?'"

"I froze," Henry tells us,

> when I beheld chains being pulled by white-like, bent-over men. On their heads were the signs of oppression. On their heads were signs of superiority, written in blood. They carried signs which read HATE, PREJUDICE, STARVATION, MASTER OF SLAVES, ROBBER and FAMILY OF THIEVES. And then I began to understand. These were they who knew not the meaning of freedom. Their tears were falling down like the rains from heaven and my eyes burned. I heard their sounds of supplication. "Free me, free me. I can no longer stand the pains. I was wrong but now I see. . . ."
>
> And then I beheld the sun smiling and then they vanished into nothingness. "This," said a voice from afar, "was the beginning of retribution."

Then on to Soulsville and a conversation with Billie Holiday:

"Before you split, Billie, sing one for me, baby," Henry asks her.

"Have mercy, J. Like, all right, I'm gonna dedicate this one to all my black brothers. You get this message back, J."

Billie begins singing, musicians falling into soft pleading harmony behind her:

> *Southern trees bear strange fruit*
> *Blood on leaves and blood at the root*
> *I remember my mother told me 'fore she passed away*
> *She said, "Billie, when I'm gone, don't forget to pray*
> *'Cause there'll be hard times, hard times, oh yeah"*
> *Yeah, who knows better than I?*

"As I descended from Soulsville," Henry says, "I heard a voice ask, 'Lady Day—Billie—where did you learn to sing like that?'"

> I heard her reply, "I'm not singing. I'm just souling to help me with living."
> Then I heard no more.
> I lifted up my eyes to see, but only the darkness greeted me. Then I heard a voice cry out in agony. "All things are possible if you only believe."
> I saw the light of truth shining all about me. This I bear witness to. I heard voices crying in the wilderness like a mighty wind lashing out against evil and injustice. The voice from heaven cried out to me: "Henry J., the time is near."

It was time for the final dream:

> Loneliness and panic overcame Henry J. His tongue stiffened and his thoughts silenced his mouth to seal the voice within that called on sorrow. But Henry J. remembered—like a prisoner who recalls confinement, like a child between youth and regret—he remembered. . . . He longed for his mother, somewhere in heaven, and he tried for a second to form a vision of his joys of infancy. But only the corpses, the darkness and the cold hands of death enfolded him. His soul was imprisoned in tears. He wanted to remove from his shoulders this weight that overpowered him, this ache of emptiness, the choking branches of torment, and safely put his arms around his mother's neck. He longed to be just a boy. . . . He longed for one single thought stronger than his memory. But not a sign nor a voice mingled with the breeze. Not even the spirits whispered to his heart. . . .
> "Who on earth could believe my story?" He walked on, trembling, asking that question all men finally ask of life. "What do you want of me?"
> Henry J. knew his journey was almost over, and as he reentered earth he spoke, saying, "Lord, you have given me power and taught me how to interpret mysteries. You are the creator

of the heavens and the earth, my guardian in this world and in the next. Let me die in submission and join the righteous, to live again. Oh Lord, remember me."

Henry then tells us what the Lord showed him:

I saw a new government and a new people, for the first America had passed into the resurrection. A new South, full with character, justice and progress. . . . I beheld men, old and young, black and white, all races, advanced in spirit, in unrestricted love, singing songs of comradeship, and I sang, too. I followed every mother's son and daughter. I listened to literature, art and science. All had changed to a new greatness, more resplendent and covered America's shore. . . . I saw God's flower garden of humanity dancing and laughing together. . . . I looked, and a new America appeared. Voices came out of the new America, saying, "Free at last! Free at last!"

Eight years before I'd scarcely owned a book. Now I had written a manuscript, one that distilled the hundreds of books I had bought since something tapped me on the shoulder that day in a Chicago used-book store. Why had I written this? I still did not know. Who might want to read it? I had no idea, and I was too insecure to ponder it. I put the manuscript in a drawer, where it would sit for years.

By the end of '63 my New York days were coming to an end. Either I burned out a station in a couple years, or it burned out me. There was always a better offer. This time it came from Chicago. Chess Records owned a radio station there, and Leonard Chess was willing to pay me three times what I was making in New York. In retrospect, I got out of the Apple at a good time. Remember, I was already shouting "Burn, baby! Burn!" and it wasn't long after I left New York that deadly rioting and fires broke out there in 1964. It occurred to me I'd dodged a bullet: I'd almost been shouting "Burn, baby! Burn!" in a city where a race riot started. Imagine that.

8 The Man

I hung out with Sam Cooke one last time before I left New York. He came by WWRL on Long Island in 1963, around the time he was re-cording "A Change Is Gonna Come," a record he had been in-spired to write after hearing Bob Dylan's "Blowin' in the Wind." Sam had abandoned gospel after six years of stardom with the Soul Stir-rers when he crossed over to the pop world in 1957 by recording "You Send Me." But Sam's spiritual-ity always colored his lyrics and his voice, and in its resoluteness, "A Change Is Gonna Come" was as close to God's word as any declara-tion of righteousness ever made inside a church:

> *There's been times I thought I*
> *   couldn't last too long*
> *Now I think I'm able to carry on*
> *It's been a long time coming*
> *But I know a change is gonna come.*

Sam could write the simplest lyric with such cool, smooth, elegant diction and regard for the melody that even words you would dismiss as corny ("A grape was made to grow on a vine / An apple was made to grow on a tree / As sure as there are stars above / You were made for me") fit when he wrapped his voice around them. He was the most learned, earnest, creative, spiritual—flat-out, the most talented man in the music business I ever met. Sam Cooke was more than a singer. He was a rhapsodist. Anybody else who came on the air with me had to play second fiddle, but I was honored by Sam's presence.

"Good afternoon, darlings," I said to my listeners on this day. "This is Magnificent Montague. And here in the studio we have a man who calls himself Mister Soul. He claims he's a singer and he claims he has a background that makes him eligible to be part of your show, darling. His name is Sam Cooke—Mister Soul."

Sam: Well, that's very simple to do to such a soulful one, Montague. Believe me, *very* easy to do. But I want to say that knowing you as long as I have, I've had a chance to even sit back and observe you. You understand?

Montague: Mmmmm. I see. In other words you've been trying to gather some material for *your* soul through mine [we both laughed].

Sam [still laughing]: I have no retort, no retort for that.

Montague: Well, Sam, tell me this. Have you changed any during the years? You look a little older, a little thinner.

Sam: Well, no, I haven't changed that much, Montague. [He smiled back.] I'll say, you know, as a singer grows older, his conception goes a little deeper because he lives life and he understands what he's trying to say a little more. If a singer tries to find out what's happening in life, it gives him a better insight on telling the story of the song he's trying to sing.

I asked him to play a game. "Pick your favorite record and recite the first line."

He chose a song I gave you a snatch of a second ago, "You Were Made for Me" and said: "A fish was made to swim in the ocean / A boat was made to sail on the sea / But sure as there are stars above, / you were made for me."

Montague: And I can recap that by saying, of all the fish in the ocean, of all the waves on the sea, there's nothing, darling, that I could bait more better than you and me. And being the captain of my ship, I know that wherever I sail, darling, you were made for me. How did you like that, Sam?

Sam: You know, Montague, I think we must get together and collaborate at least once on a song.

Montague: That would be terrific. What's your second-best record?

Sam: My second-best record—well, I love my current one very much, called "Nothing Can Change This Love."

Montague: All right, now, we'll see if we can do like we did before and I'll see if I can come up with something.

Sam: All right, this says, uh, "If I go a million miles away, I'd write a letter and every day, 'cause nothing can change the love I have for you."

Montague: If I should go beyond the clouds, beyond the world renown, if I should in my sleep stumble out loud, darling I am not afraid to write your name a thousand times. For nothing in this crazy world can change my love. I know, thank God, that nothing can change my love for you. Well, Sam, how'd you like that? [We both laughed.]

Sam: That was nice, Montague, but you know I can't cap that.

Montague: No, no, no, I wasn't trying to get you to cap that. I was merely looking at you, trying to observe. And I think that to close the show up very nicely, Sam, I would like for you to . . . to hum something, just slightly. You hum something for my darlings. In other words, every day I try to describe "soul." Maybe you can hum eight bars of what soul represents. [Sam began to hum, a sound that put me at peace.] And when the humming's over, and time finds its soul, all I can

say to you, darling, is "Sam Cooke's yours. He'll never grow
old." Sam, it's been nice.
Sam: It's been wonderful.

Of course, Sam Cooke never did grow old. He would be dead at
thirty-three in less than a year, shot in a tragic misunderstanding.
When a contemporary (Sam was three years younger than me) dies
violently, when someone whose talent leaves you awestruck has
his life snuffed out that young, when someone you were counting
on to go through life with as an inspiration is taken away from you,
it hurts in indescribable ways. It still hurts. As I write this, Sam has
been dead exactly as long as he was alive—and you still hear his
music, his lyrics, his beautiful soul, which infiltrated its way into
so many crevices of popular music. That may, indeed, be enough
for you, or for his legacy, but it is not enough for me, because I
know how Sam would have put his stamp on every music fan, of
every race, had he lived the life he deserved. He was the bridge—
he would have been the widest bridge—connecting the exhausted,
prayerful melodies of the first black slave to the deep sigh or moan
or scream of the last black singer you heard the last time you turned
on your car radio. Sam's voice—Sam's being—reached across three
hundred years, reached effortlessly into the spiritual world of our
people, and walked into the popular world without compromising.
By example and by the gift of teaching, he set the standard for
hundreds of others to follow the way. Jerry Butler and Curtis
Mayfield owe Sam. Wilson Pickett and Otis Redding and Sam and
Dave owe him. Johnnie Taylor and Bobby Womack, who recorded
on the SAR label, which Sam created just two years after moving
into the pop world, owe him. Al Green, Prince, Mariah Carey—
anybody you can name, anybody who sang in a church or was
influenced by anybody who sang in a church, owes Sam because
it was Sam, in the early sixties, who showed us how to lift the rising, majestic feeling that swirls within the music of the Negro
church and apply it to rhythm and blues. He was not the first, but

he was by far the best. And, befitting the soul tradition, his mastery was not merely technical; it was personal.

Sam was a creation of the Lord that happens every few generations. Oh, it will happen again, probably not in my lifetime, but it will happen: God will send down another chosen songster to blend spiritual and secular music, with the lyrical phraseology to interpret biblical personages in the twenty-first century. Like the wind bent the trees, Sam bent the notes. Like the ocean's calm, Sam's was the celestial pause. He was anointed, and everybody he touched knew it. He and his music were one. He came at you with no musical gimmicks, no rewrites, no difficult lyrics, just a little old guitar he plucked that wasn't bigger than a candy box, a small toy-looking thing he had to help him compose and demonstrate his ideas. Couldn't change keys and didn't need to. His guitar was just there for rhythm. He was the instrument. Come session time, he'd bring in his guitar man, Cliff White. ("Cliff, play with all your fervor," you can hear Sam command on a Soul Stirrers cut he produced on SAR after leaving the group.) Sam's melodies were spontaneous chordal colors, springing to life like the Negro spirituals of a century before—seemingly ready-made, generated during some protracted meeting in a work camp or a church, riding on the power of rhythm and spirit. In all spirituals there breathes a hope, a faith in the ultimate justice and brotherhood of man. The cadences of sorrow invariably turn to joy. And so it was, always, with Sam.

There's a wonderful Stax song that came out in 1966, a couple years after Sam's death, called "Soothe Me." A Sam and Dave record. I loved to play it on the radio, loved the way their voices played off each other like they would in church, challenging and shaping each other, almost calling out to one another and answering. The song was a tribute to Sam. He'd originally produced it for a duo called the Simms Twins, who were performing both gospel and R&B in churches and clubs. Sam had used the twins as backup singers on "Cupid" in '61 and was so taken with their ability to replicate a larger group of singers that he wrote "Soothe Me" for them to record for SAR. Then Sam gave the same song to the Soul Stirrers, who were also on SAR, so they could turn around the words and call it "Lead Me, Jesus." In the pop world the song began this way:

Soothe me baby, soothe me.
Soothe me with your kindness
For you know your powerful loving
Is soothing to me.

In the gospel world it began

Lead me, Jesus, lead me.
Lead me through the darkness.
If you lead me to the light,
Everything's gonna be all right.

In the nineties Allen Klein, Sam's manager, completed a labor of love and released the SAR catalog as a double CD, along with some reminiscences, including one about the tension between those two versions of the song. Le Roy Crume, the Soul Stirrers' guitarist and baritone singer, remembered:

Sam told me, "Le Roy, I got a hit coming out, 'Soothe Me.'" And he said, "I want you to write a gospel to it." I said, "You're not going to let your R&B number come out first?" He said, "Oh, no, I'll hold it." [But] man, that R&B [version] came out before our record, and I said, "Sam, why you do that?"

Man, we played Atlanta and the promoter was standing out on the steps and he didn't even say hello or nothing, he just said, "Crume, why in the world did you guys do that?" I said, "What, man? What are you talking about?" He said, "This rock 'n' roll song. You all recorded a rock 'n' roll song." I said, "No, man, we didn't record a rock 'n' roll song." He said, "Well, it's just like a rock 'n' roll song. It's not going to work, man." He said, "You guys used to be #1 here, but you can forget it. Man, you might get booed off the stage."

Oh, man, I was so scared. That was the one time I took [lead singer] Jimmie [Outler] in the dressing room and said, "Jimmie, let's don't even touch that song." I said, "Just sing one line, and let's walk." Well, that's what we did, and, man, the crowd just went crazy, and the promoter came to me and said, "Damn, you guys can do anything you want!"

We met originally, Sam and me, after I put his younger brother L. C. into the Magnificents. Sam's father, Bishop Cooke, who lived to be ninety-nine, moved the family from Mississippi to Chicago when Sam was two. As children, Sam, L. C., and the other siblings performed as a gospel group. Then, at fifteen, Sam became lead singer of a teenage gospel group. Finally, at nineteen, in 1950, he was handpicked to replace R. H. Harris as the Soul Stirrers' lead singer. This was sort of like replacing Franklin D. Roosevelt as president: Harris, who had a gruffer voice than Sam (but an awesome one—it cut through you with the power of God's left hook), had been fronting the Soul Stirrers since they were founded five years before Sam was born.

For six years women at gospel concerts screamed for Sam, for his polish and his passion and his sheer gift. For the next six years women at his pop concerts did the same. He recorded or wrote twenty-nine Top-40 hits, from "You Send Me" to "Bring It on Home to Me," "Another Saturday Night," "Chain Gang," and "Everybody Likes to Cha Cha Cha," which he dashed off in a couple minutes at a Christmas party as he watched the folks dance. He was immediately and naturally as attractive to white audiences, partly because his melodies were so accessible, his lyrics were so polished, and his enunciation was—man, I never heard anybody talk like Sam. Nat King Cole couldn't touch him. Nat's diction was manufactured. Sam's was like Harvey's Bristol Cream versus Manischewitz. Everything he said was like poetry.

Sam loved to read, loved knowledge. Like Malcolm X, he was fascinated by my collection, by the idea that someone would have a hobby like that. He had a standing joke when he visited me and Rose. He'd see something from the collection and say: "Montague, is this for me?" He loved our race. Dunbar was his favorite black poet, for the dialect poetry. "You know," he told me once, "Dunbar is a balladeer. His phrases and nuances act out the soul of black folks." He picked up his little guitar and started strumming a few chords and sang a couple verses of "When Malindy Sings":

Fiddlin' man jes' stop his fiddlin'
Lay his fiddle on de she'f
Mockin'-bird quit tryin' to whistle
'Cause he jes' so shamed hisse'f.

He wasn't reading from anything. He knew it as the day is long. I loaned him one of my books on Dunbar, and he leafed through it, reading the dialect without a stumble or a pause. I couldn't do that! He could do it because the cadence was religious, the meter was faithful to how the people who'd written those gospel songs talked.

Preacher, poet, rapper—Sam was all these things. Where did he get it? He got it from Daddy Cooke, who got it from his father. It was passed from slavery, from those certain tunes, certain messages, that formed the core of our spirituals. Sam's house was one of the few places where I ever shut up. I listened to Papa. Why? Because as much history as I knew, Papa knew more. Sam and his father had the same soul. Sam understood the passage from slavery to the South and the movement to freedom so much better than I did. I understood it through osmosis, academically; he had felt it every day of his life, and you heard it in every note he wrote or sang. He was in the forefront of the black experience years before anybody used that term. Whatever came out of his mouth, you heard your antecedents.

My love for Sam—my worshipful appreciation of him—spills out often when I run my hands over my collection. He connects me to the people who were dead a century before I came across their legacies. I'm thinking about a collecting trip in Los Cruces, New Mexico, in 1970, when I walked into a rare-book shop and, praise the Lord, something moved me at the door. To the left was an old stack of boxes. I looked up on top, and the book's title page was there before my eyes: *Slave Songs of the United States,* published 1867. In mint condition. My nervous fingers lightly turned the pages. The owner said he had yet to catalog or price anything in the box. "What's that book doing out?" he said. He threw out a ridiculous quote, several thousand dollars, but automatically, something inside me told me to say yes. I walked out with it, back to the car, on cloud nine. This was the first original book of Negro plantation spirituals I had ever found in more than ten years of hard-core collecting. I cherished these songs because they told the story of plantation days. They were called *sperichils* (in dialect) and chants, taken down right after the Civil War and fit into notes as close as the music could fit. There was one called "Run, Nigger, Run." There was "Michael Row the Boat Ashore." There was a classic song that I never knew came from Negro folklore, "Buffalo Gals."

A lot of chants were sung by black stevedores of the West Indian vessels who came to the South and loaded and unloaded in places like Port Royal, South Carolina, and Savannah, Georgia. So we not only had the spirituals, but we had the secular melodies, too. When they wanted leisure-time songs, they just changed the words—just like Sam would do—and came up with fiddle songs, devil songs, shout and coon songs.

It's impossible for me to sift through that part of Negro history without missing Sam. It's also impossible to ignore a fact that he appreciated, which explained his crossover strength, both from gospel to pop and from black to white. Ask yourself who took down those slave songs and transferred them to sheet music? Whites. In fact, who published all the books in my collection written by blacks? Whites. If those whites hadn't published 'em, there'd be no history.

Sam was so good, so refined, so spiritual, he seemed almost not of this world, like Doctor King. It was that quality of being anointed. Both of them were comfortable—probably far more than they should have been—walking into dangerous circumstances. Both reached back to the Bible to tell a contemporary story, like minstrels who tell the story back to the rhapsody. Sam didn't talk any hate, he didn't talk aggressive, I never heard him cuss, and—in sharp contrast to the circumstances of his death—I never heard him talk about chasing women. Never heard Sam switch in and out of black or white talk, either. Other artists, you'd have to gear yourself when you talked to them, depending if you were on or off the air. Sam was always himself. The closest to Sam in that regard was Otis Redding. Yeah, Otis reminded me of Sam. Beautiful soul, great smile, that Negro spiritual feeling. (Otis's version of "A Change Is Gonna Come," which he recorded in 1965, the same year Sam's original was released, is even more powerful.)

When he was twenty-eight, Sam started his own L.A.-based record label, SAR, putting his extraordinary teaching talent on display. He pulled together the best talent on the West Coast: the Simms Twins; Bobby Womack and his brothers, who also became the Valentinos (the Rolling Stones grabbed the Valentinos' "It's All Over Now" a couple months after it was released in '64, and the J. Geils Band covered the Valentinos' "Lookin' for a Love" a few years later); Billy Preston; Johnnie Morisette; the great Johnnie Taylor; and Mel Carter. Plus, Sam kept producing gospel by the Soul Stirrers and the Womack Brothers. He always knew what he wanted, always knew the precise arrangement, the right lilt or growl of the voice. You can hear him on *Sam Cooke's SAR Records Story,* the 1994 double CD, lecturing the Soul Stirrers about making sure of their grammar, right down to the appropriate use of *thine.* God bless Allen Klein for his obsession with packaging and releasing those recordings. Allen is determined to produce a movie about Sam's life. I'm not sure I could watch it, though, because there would be no way to write around the ending.

I was in Chicago in December 1964 when Sam died. Three months earlier I had been fired from WVON, the station owned by Leonard Chess, who'd lured me back a year before from New York. Leonard had courted me back then, picking up Rose at the airport and showing her the best place to live downtown. She signed a lease at Carl Sandburg Village, a big new apartment building that had yet to have a black resident. (This was something that never

changed: Rose always leased every place we lived. She was the anchor of the family, and I wasn't going to be trapped by the feeling
that I had to live in a black neighborhood just because of my race.)

If you want to know the kind of world the independent record
companies ran, check this out. I had opened up a record shop with
another WVON deejay, Rodney Jones, and I'd gotten some financial assistance from Don Robey in Houston and Berry Gordy in
Detroit, both of whom I had business relationships with. Leonard
was pissed off about that because Robey had sued him over the use
of an album by the Five Blind Boys. So Leonard comes to me and
Rodney and says, in effect: "You guys took payola from Robey and
Gordy, but I'll let it slide if you sign this affidavit saying Robey paid
you off, because that will make Robey drop his damn lawsuit
against me." To which I said: "Leonard, fuck you." But it was harder
for Rodney, because Chess held the mortgage to his house; Chess
had created WVON as a black-oriented station with black jockeys
to play Chess (and sometimes other companies') records. Share-
croppin' was still alive and well. And now a white man who is stealing from blacks wants to use two blacks—us—to trap two of the
biggest black record makers in America.

After I got fired, I got a call from Jim Randolph, the black program director of white-owned KGFJ in Los Angeles. We'd worked
together at KSAN in San Francisco. There was a spot open if I wanted
it. I said yes. When I told Berry Gordy I was moving west, he was so
grateful for the way I had stood up to Leonard Chess that he paid
my moving charges. In fact, Atlantic Records, which was distribut-
ing "Mercy, Mercy," a Top-10 hit I had produced for Don Covay in
New York the year before, also paid my moving charges because the
record was selling so well. (We put that out on a label I created,
Rosemart, named for my wife and our son, Martin, and it didn't
hurt that those cagey Rolling Stones made a hit out of "Mercy,
Mercy" in '64, the same way they'd hit with the Valentinos' "It's All
Over Now.") In fact, a few other record companies also took care of
my moving charges to L.A. I made a profit before I even got there.

Sam was delighted when I told him I was coming. I'd been

broadcasting ten years straight, and I was going to turn thirty-
seven soon. We talked about jointly buying a radio station. "We
need to buy one, Montague," he said.

L. C. Cooke telephoned me. I thought he was calling about setting up some rehearsals.

Sam got shot to death, he said.

It was like hearing about the Kennedy assassination thirteen
months earlier. This made just as little sense.

The way the police told it, Sam had met a young singer in a Hollywood celebrity hangout, offered her a ride to the Hollywood motel where she lived, but instead took her to a motel in South Los
Angeles. Once there, the girl said, he tore off her clothes. She escaped from the room, grabbing her clothes and, inadvertently, his
pants, and went to call the police. Sam went to the manager's unit
demanding to look for the girl, broke down the door, and struggled
with the manager until the manager grabbed a .22 off the top of the
TV and shot him. The authorities would rule it justifiable homicide.
It was hard for me to work up the nerve to go see Bishop Cooke.

None of this was fathomable, and it was more comforting to
believe, as some fans did, that this had been a mob hit. What difference did it make? I flew to Los Angeles for the funeral at Mount
Sinai Baptist Church, where thousands waited hours to hear Ray
Charles, Lou Rawls, and Bobby "Blue" Bland sing (they had to carry
off a scheduled gospel singer, Bessie Griffin, when she became too
distraught to perform), and then back to Chicago for a second,
even more heartbreaking Cooke family service in that city. Soon I
was flying back to Los Angeles to sign my contract with KGFJ. I'd
start on the air in February 1965. I should been jubilant, arriving
in triumph, but all I could think of was how much I'd looked for-
ward to seeing Sam.

If you should happen to purchase that collection of SAR recordings, you will find an essay I wrote about Sam in 1971:

> In the early '50s, Sam was singing in storefront churches
> throughout the North and South. I was disc jockeying on small

radio stations also in the North and South. Our parents were shouting, singing and clapping hands in the South and then they made their exodus to the North.

Our gift of song and dance is not by chance, nor is death by chance. Man is ordained and predestined to achieve . . . [and] to suffer, but his soul is an unknown gift that only God can make. That same God, call him what you may, gave to Sam the gospel feeling and the ability to translate the sacred mysteries of black music into our American environment so that all, regardless of race, color or creed, would lend an ear and enjoy a voice that set the pace for today's trend.

Sam Cooke's yours. He'll never grow old.

Highlights of the Montague Collection: Frank Sapp's 1944 painting of the Haitian general Toussaint L'Ouverture astride a horse has long graced my residences. (*Los Angeles Times* photo by Rick Meyer)

20. *A Negro inventor: Robert Blair, inventor of anti-aircraft gun.*

◆ 238 ◆

Photograph of Robert Blair, the inventor of the antiaircraft gun.

Book of dialect poetry by Paul Laurence Dunbar.

Peanut-oil painting by George Washington Carver.

Poster advertising a performance by the Flying Negro Singers.

THE APPREHENSION OF THE FUGITIVE.

WE have seen in a previous engraving the slave flying for refuge from the accursed Fugitive Slave Law. Here we see him arrested, torn from his home, from his business, from the wife of his bosom and the children of his love. No matter how respectable and well-behaved the man may have been before, this law willingly consigned him to the wretched bondage, the worst and most degrading that can befall man. In America this is by no means an uncommon occurrence. In a former number, says the *Richmond Standard*, we gave an account of the last slave-hunt in Pennsylvania, when a man of the name of Phillips, who had for years been an industrious and respectable citizen of Harrisburg, in that state, was brutally knocked on the head, to render his capture certain, and then taken, in a state of insensibility, before Commissioner M'Allister, who mocked and insulted him with a sham trial, and delivered him over to his captors, as a slave for life. His case excited a deep feeling of indignation among the people of Harrisburg, from the manner of his capture and the character of the pretended trial which was awarded him, and also moved their sympathies for his probable fate, and for the sudden desolation which had thus fallen on his wife. The man-stealer, regardless of the misery he creates, enters a happy family, drags away the father to a felon's jail, deprives the members of that family of their natural guardian and head, and all this is done in a land that boasts that all are free.

Reproduction of an 1853 abolitionist pamphlet on slavery.

"NOW I'SE GOT SOME MONEY, I'SE A COMIN' 'ROUND"

Painting by an unknown artist of the slave "cakewalk" ritual.

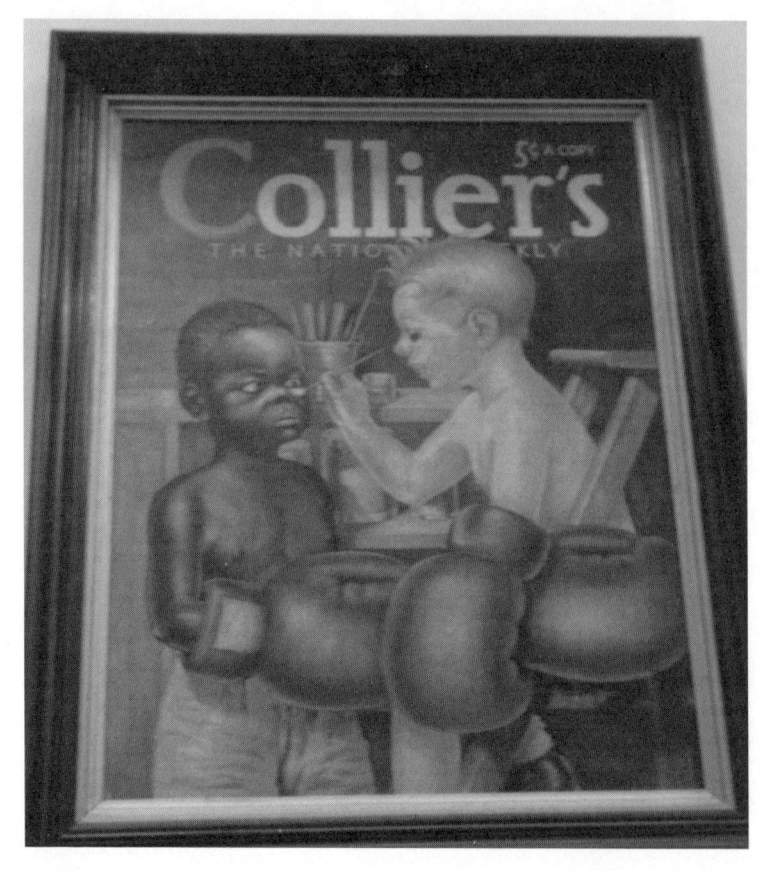

Collier's magazine cover.

Rudolf von Mehoffer's painting of African royalty, circa 1870.

With my fan-turned-collaborator Bob Baker.

With my wife of forty-eight years, Rose Catalon.

9 The Riot

Well, we're just about back where we started this story.

It's August 1965, and now we're really gonna burn.

I'm onstage, me and Wilson Pickett, on a broiling Sunday night inside the old 5-4 Ballroom at Fifty-fourth and Broadway in what's now called South-Central Los Angeles but was then known simply as the Negro area. We're one floor up a flight of wooden stairs, face to face with a crowd of screaming fans.

Pickett wants to do "Midnight Hour," which had just come out, but he has this problem: the whole Stax Records revue has been hammering the audience for a solid hour—Rufus Thomas and Booker T. and MGs and William Bell and Carla Thomas and the Mad Lads and the Mar-Keys, each of 'em pumping up the boys and girls with machine-gun-like one- and two-song sets. I'm promoting and emceeing the show, calling the musicians on and off like a track coach with a whip while the MGs back each one. I'm keeping that frantic rhythm going, jacking up the pace, trading my line with the crowd: "Burn, baby! Burn!"—shouting it on the mike during the songs, on the right beat, so it sounds like part of the mix, and the echo from that feverish congregation comes back at me a thousand times as strong: "BURRRRNNN!" Just the way they'd been screaming it at me on KGFJ every morning since I went on the air there early in the year.

So here comes Pickett, and how does he top *this?* Like any great performer, he amps up the drama. Girls in the crowd are already screaming out for "Midnight Hour," but he teases them, asking them if they believe the midnight hour is "the right time." Then, after that bit, he cries out my name, calls me to center stage, exclaiming: "Montague! I got to sing this song, Montague!" The way he shouts it puts me back in my mother's church.

"Why you got to sing it?" I shout in encouragement.

"You made it *possible* for me to sing it!" Pickett exclaims. (I damned sure made it possible, the number of times I'd been playing it.) "You told the soooooul sisters! You told the soooooul brothers! They got to wait!"

I fire back: "They got to wait!"

"They got to *waaaaait!*" Pickett continues, and then the rumbling drums of the MGs and the horns of the Mar-Keys kick in, and Pickett, in that raw voice that overtakes you like a preacher and a pimp in the same instant, busts into his hit.

There was so much energy in moments like this in L.A. that sometimes I just wanted to stand back and watch. The way these kids hungered for my signature phrase, the way they'd call up on the air—on this special "burn line" we gave them—and shout it out . . . it was like it was a declaration of their existence.

It wasn't supposed to be all that. It was just a way of paying tribute (six months before, you might have said something was "cooking"), and yet they gave it back to me with the fervor of a revival meeting. Something was passing between us that there were no words for. That radio minister I'd copied back in Texas would have been proud. I'd be throwing "Burn!" into practically every song—beginning, end, calling over the record, backing up to the last four bars and doing it again if I got excited. For the kids who called up on my morning drive show, the rules for the burn line were plain: you shouted your name, your school, and then "Burn!" Nothing else.

These days kids have every kind of T-shirt and sneakers and tattoo and jewelry to flash their identity, to make them feel special. It wasn't that way back then. If you were colored, you might as well have been anonymous. There were half a million Negroes in Los Angeles when I came back this time around, and most of their families had been there only one, maybe two generations. These families had come flooding in during the fifties and sixties, full of expectations, and wound up squashed and segregated into thirty or forty square miles that were south of downtown and way east of the beach. (KGFJ was a tiny station, 1,000 watts, with its transmitter in the San Fernando Valley, so that some parts of South-Central L.A. couldn't even get the frequency, and lots of fans would simply get into their cars and drive around so they could pick me up.)

As the colored folks came, the white folks went, heading north and west. You think of '65 and the West and you think freedom, new beginnings. You're wrong. Negro Los Angeles in '65 was no different from colored L.A. in '55. Negro L.A. could have been a poor small town: no hospitals, no subway—the trolley system had just been torn down in favor of the freeway, and buses were hard to come by. Police were almost entirely white, and the chief still sounded like he was calling us "nigras." Three months before I got there, California's voters, swayed by commercials that appealed to "property rights," had overwhelmingly repealed the state's fair-housing law. Against that backdrop, my audience responded to me the way a prison audience responds to the most charismatic inmate.

Of course this inmate wasn't in prison, at least not in the same one. I was living way to the west, in Brentwood. Never lived in a slum and wasn't about to. Over the phone, on the burn line, it was hard to see the contradictions in my audience's lives. They sounded like people in a beautiful, striving community who loved to express themselves, and yet they were quietly raging at the chains of de facto segregation, smoldering at oppression. This was not obvious to outsiders. Remember, there was no "talk radio" back then. You didn't call up and spout off. The white city saw and heard nothing of what the black side was experiencing.

Los Angeles had slapped me in the face the moment I arrived. I tried to rent an apartment for a few months at the all-white Barrington Plaza, two miles from the beach, and was told . . . well, you can imagine what I was told. I had a white friend, a record distributor named Leland Rogers, Kenny Rogers's brother, and he decided to step in. We went back there with me posing as his driver, and he rented the apartment in the name of my wife. (The first time I went out to the swimming pool with my son after we moved in, the manager caught hell; as best I can place it, that was the same month the sheriff in Selma, Alabama, beat up a bunch of civil rights marchers trying to cross a bridge during one of Doctor King's voting-rights drives.)

Because I didn't live in the 'hood, I was not aware of what happened early on Wednesday night, three nights after Pickett and I stepped off the 5-4 Ballroom stage.

I was not aware that about seventy blocks further south in the Negro area, in a place called Watts, a cop pulled over a young black man for drunk driving.

I was not aware that his mother came to the scene to claim his car.

I was not aware that a crowd gathered—first twenty-five, then fifty, then three hundred.

I was not aware that the drunk driver got ugly with the cops, that they radioed for more help, that somebody swung a nightstick, and that within a few minutes the crowd grew to one thousand.

I was not aware that somebody spat at a cop, that a false rumor spread that a pregnant woman had been struck. That brothers began pulling whites out of their cars and beating them.

By Thursday morning, at work, I knew plenty, but that wasn't going to change my style. I was burning, shouting, screaming, taking calls. At this point there was an uneasy calm on the streets. A relatively small amount of rioting had taken place a few hours after midnight. Neighborhood groups and people the newspapers liked to call "Negro leaders" held a huge, hot meeting with county human-relations officials in the afternoon, trying to hold off a riot. They put the meeting on TV, and while there were plenty of Negroes speaking out for calm, TV fell in love with the rage in the voices of some of the teenagers who grabbed the mike.

"It's like this," cried one. "The way the policemens treat you 'round here, I'm going to tell you something: it ain't gonna be lovely tonight whether you like it or not." The audience jeered him down but he wouldn't stop. "We, the Negro people, have got completely fed up. They not going to fight down here no more. . . . They going to congregate . . . everywhere the white man supposed to stay. They going to do the white man in tonight!"

Cal Milner, the operations manager, called my home that afternoon and told Rose that the police chief, William Parker, was trying to "mobilize" the Negro deejays and that I should stop saying "Burn!" I got home too late to talk to anybody.

It all busted out that Thursday night. The fires and the looting that would eventually cost $40 million. The bullets that would eventually kill thirty-five people. The "Get Whitey!" cries. The first building they burned was one near that first arrest, with cops holding back the rioters as the firemen tried to put it out.

And that was the first time I heard it with my own ears.

Going to bed, I turned on my television set and saw fire leaping to the rhythm of my phrase. It was so unreal. Buildings burning and I heard it; I heard somebody chant it: "Burn, baby! Burn!" I was sleepy, and for a moment I thought it must be a movie, somebody using my line without my permission. That had certainly happened before, with other bits. And then I saw a close-up shot of the crowd in wild, joyous ecstasy, looting, breaking into stores, and carrying radios and TVs on their heads as if they were back in Mother Africa. Screaming police kicking and beating back the crowd. The ghetto was lit up, and the refrain kept on repeating,

"Burn, baby! Burn!" I wasn't fathoming the true significance of all this, only my slogan—only the sense of my show projected bigger than ever—so I turned over and went to sleep. I had to be up at 4:30 to wake up L.A. at 6.

I got to the station Friday morning at 5:45, did my usual thing, and at 6 shouted, "Wake up, Los Angeles!" like always. I didn't have time to read no damn paper. We had UPI at the station. My job was to hit them with that churchy "Montague the Magnificent" theme song and promise them that although there was pain in their hearts, if they would just put their hand on the radio, I would save them.

I was going to do it again today.

The tape of the intro song ends and I take my first call: "My name is Helen Williams. I go to Jordan High School. Burn, baby! Burn!"

Then she adds something: "And Montague: don't you stop!"

Why should I?

I took fifteen more calls, played three records, and was waking up Los Angeles. Today I was not cutting off any comments beyond name and school, like I usually did, because I knew this was different. I had to let them vent. I was still moving through my routine. I didn't live in the riot zone or work there (the station was on Melrose, far north), and I had so much to do: get those commercials ready, run my own turntables, answer my private line, and answer the station's private line—which was now ringing.

I picked it up, and the voice over the phone said: "Stop. Don't say 'Burn, baby! Burn!'" It was Arnold Shore, the general manager and brother of KGFJ's owner.

I went off on him and made a threat I had made in Boston, Texas, Chicago, St. Louis, Denver, New York—every radio station I'd ever worked at. "You outta your mind? I'll quit!"

"But Montague! The mayor, the chief of police—they're pleading with me to stop. You're inciting! You're leading the crowd!"

He knew that wasn't true, but if you were from the white side of the city and didn't know anything about me or the show or the station, that's what you'd think. Remember the time. It was an era in which "outside agitators" were routinely blamed for every social disturbance, and there was no civil rights leader to blame for this one, no demonstration that got out of hand, nothing to explain why the burning was expanding. Nobody was about to say what they should have said, that this was a huge, unfocused protest—a rebellion, which is what you will still hear black folks call the Watts riots, as well as the Rodney King riots that hit in '92. We had a mayor back then, Sam Yorty, and a police chief, Massa' Parker, who were part of the cold-war, anticommunist school of paranoia that considered uppity Negroes part of the conspiracy to disrupt society. They needed to lynch somebody.

"No," I said. "I'm not gonna stop. It's time for people to go to work, for people to do what they usually do. You set something aside and make this a special situation with me, you're really going to create something. You're going to make me lose my credibility. And I'm not about to lose my credibility just 'cause I'm a Negro, just 'cause I'm their leader on the radio, and all they want to do is say, 'Burn, baby! Burn!' For me to stop it is to say they're wrong and the Establishment is right and that I'm an Uncle Tom and I go along with it."

I was furious. The slogan, this delightful thing, belonged to my listeners. It was theirs! A part of them. How was I going to take that away from them? How could anybody presume this could make them start or stop the burning? TV is already reporting the use of the phrase—doesn't know where it came from, doesn't care. They need a reason, and they'll take the simplest one; they couldn't fathom the complexities that are causing this—and truthfully, maybe neither can I at the moment, but at least I'm not pretending I can.

I thought of something else.

"You know," I told the owner, "I have not received any calls from the mothers and the fathers for me to stop. Tell you what I'll do: I'll put out a call-and-respond message, for only mothers and fathers to call me for the next fifteen minutes to see if they're in agreement. Then you call me back in a half-hour and I'll let you know. Listen to your own station! Ain't no use you coming down here now to pull me off the air in your pajamas."

What the owner didn't know—what nobody but the other jocks in the station knew—was that I had him on the air during this whole conversation. It was a measure of protection. It was a stick up his ass. Hey, it was a black-oriented station! A station that was supposed to be loving blacks, serving them.

So I put out the call. Mothers, I said, call me. If you want me to stop saying, "Burn, baby! Burn!" tell me. If you want me to say it, tell me. Tell me your name and your child's name and school. You only got thirty seconds with the music under you, otherwise I cut you off.

Phone rings.

"I'm Estelle Johnson, my daughter attends John Muir Junior High School, her name is Betty. Keep on burnin', Montague!"

I took about a dozen calls like that. Then I took about a dozen of the kids' calls.

That didn't stop the pressure.

Now Mayor Yorty himself calls up, and the owner puts him through to me. There's another song playing when I talk to him. We talk privately.

"You know," Yorty says in his midwestern twang, "there's a riot going on, and you're very popular among the Negroes. And we'd like to ask you if you can stop using that term, because it tends to incite them."

"I beg your pardon," I said. "What incites them is their problems over there. What incites them is what you white people have been doing. . . . Don't waste your time on me."

"Well, we'll have to talk to the owners again."

"They're listening. It's a three-way line."

"Well, Montague, we'll have to tell the engineer to take you off the air."

"Well, then you'll have to have to tell the people who're listening—and then you'll really have a problem."

It was touch and go because I didn't want to get Negroes to feel

I could be forced into that position. I didn't care about this piece-of-tail job. I wasn't getting rich off the pay. I made my money with the side benefits, and I could do that anywhere.

I called Rose at home. "What do you think?" I asked.

"Montague," she said, with great calm in her voice, the way there always was, "don't get involved in telling them what to do about the riot. They're your listeners. They have minds of their own. Your job is to entertain, to keep 'em happy."

After I got off the air at noon Friday, I got in my car and drove to Watts. I wanted to see for myself.

I had gotten some calls from a group called the Sons of Watts, young men who moved easily through the Negro community and understood its frustrations. With them, I toured Broadway, Santa Barbara (today it's Martin Luther King Boulevard), Western, Vermont, Firestone, and Florence. I talked with my listeners. On approaching them, up came the fingers—riot code. One meant you were from Watts, two meant Compton, and three meant Willowbrook, an area next to Watts. I saw a lot of smiles and heard the greeting: "Burn, baby! Burn!" Everybody was cool. Some were rummaging through stores, looking for items to take home. Some were dancing in the street. Some were still being chased by police. It was odd, watching people loot and jump with jubilance. They were just as happy, just as joyful, as when they would call me every morning when I would say, "Can I get a witness?" They saw me now, flashed their fingers, yelled the salutation, and told me their names. If they had something in their hands, they would put it down, come over, and shake my hand. They didn't ask me if I thought they were wrong or right. We didn't have no political discussion. I was out there because I felt that I had to go and see for myself what my listeners were going through.

This night was the worst of the rioting, the night when it seemed like it would go on forever. I could not sleep when I got home. The television set was making it seem like this was unprecedented, that it happened out of nowhere, that it made no sense, that the Negroes were crazy, mindless savages. I knew, from collecting, something that TV would never tell: race riots went as far back in this country as black folks themselves. As far back as 1663, when the Negro slaves rebelled in Gloucester, Virginia. Back to 1712, when a slave revolt in New York killed nine whites and resulted in the execution of twenty-one slaves. Back to 1741, in the British colony of New York, when white hysteria broke out over fears that slaves might betray Britain in its war against Spain. They burned thirteen slaves alive and hung another eighteen. Back to 1906, when Negro soldiers raided Brownsville, Texas, in protest against racial insults. And in East St. Louis. And Houston. All the way up to what'd happened the previous summer after I left the air in New York: riots in Harlem, Rochester—even my hometown of Elizabeth, New Jersey. Nothing special about what was going on this Friday the thirteenth of August. Most of it was just another television special. This was when Negroes got their prime-time shot. I played this over and over and over in my mind until dawn . . . and the burning went on. I was going back on the air Monday. What was I going to do?

Saturday it started to look like things were going to wind down. The National Guard had been called in Friday, and some of the energy was beginning to play itself out. My radio station was broadcasting editorials condemning the violence. "Come off the streets," it was urging.

And then came Sunday and my cover was blown. On the front page of the *Los Angeles Times* was the headline:

"Burn, Baby, Burn" Slogan Used
as Firebugs Put Area to Torch

Above the headline was the kicker: "Password Gains Safe Passage."

It's either funny or tragic: the *Times* had no Negro reporters, and the white ones were getting the hell beaten out of them, so they found a young black ad salesman, sent him out to the ghetto, and had him phone in his observations to a white rewrite man. His first paragraph reported: "Negro arsonists raced autos through otherwise deserted Los Angeles streets, flinging Molotov cocktails into store after store and shouting a hep slogan borrowed from a radio disc jockey: 'Burn, baby, burn!'"

I was not expecting the white press to catch on to this. I was not unhappy they had, but this obviously put more pressure on me, gave heat to the impression that I was inciting all this. The article never mentioned me or the station or the fact that "Burn!" had nothing to do with rioting—which meant it just fed into white people's worst fears. The reporter concluded the story of driving through the streets on Friday night by saying:

> But I was hep by that time. Whenever a group of Negroes approached to look me over, I knew what to do.
> You put your head out, and shout, "Burn, baby, burn." Then you are safe.

And now came Monday.

The alarm rang at 4:30, and I had some business to take care of.

Garbage was piling up in Watts and South L.A. because sanitation workers were afraid to collect it. A hundred schools whose playgrounds were supposed to be open in summer were shut down. Bus service was shut down. More than ten thousand troops patrolled the Negro area. Like a drunk awaking, Los Angeles looked at itself, shook its head, and winced. The streets were relatively quiet. The governor declared that the rioting and looting had ended. A curfew stayed in place.

Rose had reminded me to respect my listeners. "Voice your opinion with discretion," she'd said over the weekend. "Maybe you can come up with something else to say to keep your show rolling without anybody thinking you're some Uncle Tom, that you got backed off, because they know you're a tough man."

And right there I knew what I was going to do.

I had another phone line that I used, a separate call-in line. We called it the "have-mercy" line, and we used it at different times of the day or for different segments.

That morning I signed on a new way.

"Have mercy, Los Angeles!" I shouted, and I told my listeners that "Have mercy" was now the word. They started calling in: Montague, they asked, how do you feel about what we're doing? I tried to be fair. Segregation is not new, I told them. Discrimination is not new. The problems of the Negro community are not new. Riots ain't never been new. Love and happiness should be the tune. Do what you gotta do. Now, blacks understand that. I don't have to explain any more. "Do what you gotta do." Malcolm X said do whatever is necessary, but I'm not into politics. I'm not into leading that way. Do what you gotta do, and that's all. That was the only role I had. All day long I shouted my new slogan, like a prayer: "Have mercy, Los Angeles!" Have mercy on me for the way I love the record I'm playing. Have mercy on all of us; may we walk through this fire into better times. Be grateful, white folks, that we *had* mercy—that we stopped when we did. You could interpret it however you wanted. I kept knocking that music out heavy in between, feeding them my occasional love poetry, same as always, never mentioning anything else about what was going on. Soon they weren't, either. It was over. They'd made their point.

It was very hard for me. I did not want to stop using "Burn, baby! Burn!" any more than Merlin would have wanted to stop using magic. But it was a white-owned station, managed by whites, under pressure from the government, under pressure from the FCC. I didn't own the license, and they would have put me off the air—I knew it. I wanted to control my destiny. I wanted to respect my dignity and my listeners', and in the end I respected both. I knew my people! I'd only been in town a little while, I didn't know one street from another on the South side, and I only knew these people from the telephone, but it was a love affair. Nobody else was giving them a voice—not the NAACP, not the preachers, not my station's other deejays. But just like a song, you have to give 'em a refrain to make 'em accept it, because they won't do anything they don't want to do. The Negro church was telling them it was wrong to burn. I wouldn't do that. I knew what they were feeling. I knew they felt weak, and I knew the rioting made them feel powerful for once in their lives—that's why, again, we call it a rebellion, not against a certain policy or a particular law, but against weakness. Maybe they didn't know what they wanted. Maybe they only knew what they *didn't* want, what they would not stand for. It was a start.

Two days later, on Wednesday, a week after that drunk-driving arrest threw a match on everything, Doctor King came to town. Mayor Yorty refused to let him visit the jail where many looting and rioting suspects were being held, saying he was afraid King would set off another riot. On to Watts King went, to tour. He didn't have any better luck on the Negro side. Several hundred folks surrounded him. It was very tense. There were a lot of jeers. King had publicly called for law enforcement to suppress the rioting, and now Negroes were confronting him: What *else* could our people do, they asked, with no jobs and no prospects?

King began to speak in that marvelous voice, demanding massive government programs to help the Negro, to make sure riots did not occur again.

"We must join hands!" he said.

"And *burn!*" someone shouted from the crowd, which laughed.

There would be a better day, King told them. Somebody shouted a tough question at him: "When?" Others began to scream the watchword again: "Burn, baby! Burn!"

The tour could not continue. King left Watts.

That week the governor announced he was forming a commission to study the problem. At one of the public meetings in Watts, one of the governor's appointees, a rich Republican businessman, showed up at 103d and Grape Streets . . . in a chauffeur-driven limousine.

10 The Residue

My slogan would be stolen from me hundreds of times, made indelible not just by the brothers in the street but by one advertising agency after another and one political movement after another. The *Los Angeles Times* cartoonist Paul Conrad would immortalize it in 1966, showing the Apollo astronauts looking down on Earth, seeing the words "Burn, baby! Burn!" erupting from the planet, and saying to each other, "We're over either Cleveland, Chicago, New York or Jacksonville." Left-wing demonstrators would chant it when they burned the American flag in the seventies. Right-wing demonstrators would chant it when they stood outside prisons and cheered the use of the electric chair in the eighties. A damn disco group would steal "Burn, baby! Burn!" for the title of a song and make a big hit out of it. After the Berlin Wall fell, folks in Russia would use it in a demonstration. Nobody would ever shout it the innocent way it was supposed to be used, to praise another person's performance.

None of my doing, I kept telling myself as explosive 1965 turned into edgy 1966. I don't think you could find a year that had as much political and artistic tension rolled together as '66, and it was obvious how much the two were pushing each other. Take the tension of the Vietnam War, where an all-out escalation was now in its second year, and of the first sizable street demonstrations held in response to it; mix this with the tension over whether the passage of the civil rights bills of '64 and '65 were making the Negro's lot better. Take the tension over whether we should call ourselves Negro or black; mix it with the tension between King's Southern Christian Leadership Conference and the emerging Student Nonviolent Coordinating Committee, which was pushing King with everything but a hand in the back to go faster, to demand more, to be more confrontational. In L.A. add the additional tension over whether the riot had changed anything—whether we got anybody's attention.

Now get out your old turntable and listen to the soul music of 1966. Listen to Slim Harpo sing "Baby Scratch My Back" and Sam and Dave sing "Hold On! I'm Comin'" and Lee Dorsey sing "Working in the Coal Mine" and Stevie Wonder sing "Uptight" or "I Was Made to Love Her" and Percy Sledge sing "When a Man Loves a Woman" and Wilson Pickett sing "634-5789" and Junior Walker sing "Road Runner" and Eddie Floyd sing "Knock on Wood" and Otis Redding sing "Try a Little Tenderness" and the Capitols sing "Cool Jerk." Listen to how, even though the melodies stay in church, rapturous, the pressure is rising, as though the performers are testing you—challenging you, demanding you listen. The horn arrangements are even sharper, a little more forceful. The rhythm, out of the box, is a little faster, more dramatic. The combined effect is overwhelming. You can't sit still. The singer and the arrangement are tugging at you, wanting to make your head explode. The song builds and builds until the singer comes back after the chorus and hits the third stanza with a scream, a desire to release, to crawl out of the tensions that imprison him, to take you with him. It's like a riot, a controlled, melodious riot that is just about to break. It would break, by '68, the year that James Brown let the funk machine run wild and released "I'm Black and I'm Proud" and turned our music away from church. We weren't at that point in '66, but we were close to the edge, closer than we realized. The only place you don't feel the tension in the music of 1966 is in Detroit, where Berry Gordy is managing to go the other way and make Motown less black, less tense, and more controlled (with the exception of the rebellious Stevie Wonder) than it used to be. Berry is such a great producer that, like a scientist, he's figured out that if he keeps the vanilla on the top and the black on the bottom of his arrangements, he can increase the white cross-over audience that has already made Motown a phenomenon since '64—he can keep his people on the Ed Sullivan Show. So the performers' dance steps stay sweet and soft: no tension there. The beat stays elemental, unchallenging: no tension there. The arrangements get more orchestral, more lush: no tension there—and as a result, to many white folks, Motown becomes more and more accessible while soul music starts to feel a wee bit alienating. For every white person who might stumble across Otis Redding proposing marriage to his girlfriend while they're sitting on her couch at 3 in the morning, as in "Cigarettes and Coffee," a hundred other whites are tapping their feet or trying to dance to the Supremes crooning "You Can't Hurry Love." Talk about tension— '66 was the year James Brown appeared on the Sullivan show for the first time, dropping to his knees through "Please, Please, Please," being led off stage, weak-legged, under his cape by the Famous Flames, only to throw off the cape and run back out and sing another chorus—and then repeat the bit, and repeat it again! It was the blackest moment, racially speaking, in the history of television. And it's not just black folks feeling the tension. Listen to the Beatles' *Revolver,* breaking apart so much of the sweetness of their previous album, *Rubber Soul,* testing the limits, stretching the form, trying to make your head explode.

All of which made for great radio . . . except for the occasional moment during my L.A. morning show when a kid would call the dedication line, and instead of screaming "Have mercy, Montague!" like I had taught them since last August, he'd shout "Burn, baby! Burn!" and I'd have to make it clear that we didn't *say* that anymore, that we weren't burning anymore.

Well, not exactly.

Seven months after Watts burned, people started to notice little clusters of Negro youths on 103d Street in the riot area, just gatherings, nothing going down. Then a Mexican-American boy shot and wounded a Negro boy, and the next day a Negro adult threw a rock through the windshield of the car of a white teacher leaving a Watts high school. When the cops caught up with the rock thrower, some other brothers started yelling about police brutality, and hundreds of students and other blacks started tearing things up. The police came down hard, but not before two people died and two dozen more got hurt in several hours of looting and burning. I kept waiting to hear "Burn!" thrown around, but apparently this was not the time. (You look at the next day's newspaper, and right next to the mini-riot story with its banner headline is another reporting that President Johnson signed a bill to impose $6 billion in higher taxes to finance his goddamn war. Yes, there was an edge out there, all right.)

Two months later a young black man named Deadwyler thought his pregnant wife was in labor. (Turned out she had kidney pains.) He put her in the car to drive her to the hospital, tried to outrun the cops who wanted to pull him over, and got shot to death. If you're remembering Rodney King, I've got a few parallels for you: Deadwyler was drunk, there was a tape of the police conduct (audio), and Los Angeles was transfixed by the televised legal proceedings. And who was the unexpected star of the show? A young black attorney representing the Deadwyler family named Johnnie Cochran. The killing, coming this soon after the '65 riots, was loaded with questions about community tensions and simple justice. (This would be one of those cases that would prompt blacks to look at each other and ask, rhetorically: Is it justice? Or is it just *us*?) Authorities made the stunning decision to televise the necessary coroner's inquest into Deadwyler's death, and for eight days the black community seemed to hang on every word. It was the first big case for Cochran, who later filed an unsuccessful lawsuit against the L.A. police department on behalf of the family. The inquest jury voted six to three that the death was an accidental homicide, twisting that wedge between black and white further into our flesh, sharpening that edge.

I could feel my audience develop an edginess of its own, as though it had been empowered by the riot. Devastated, certainly (gone, among so many other buildings, was the 5-4 Ballroom), but more in control. I don't expect that to make sense to some of you, but that's what it felt like. Whenever I wanted to test a dub from a record company, or an instrumental recording that I'd made in the studio, I let the listeners decide on the weekly "Soul Time" half-hour. I'd start playing the cut and tell 'em to call and to tell me either to flush it down the toilet (using sound effects) or back it up and play four more bars. You could squeeze in one or two dozen votes on the air as the record played. Then I'd total 'em and give the record one giant flush or back it up.

One of the cuts they went nuts over was another of those half-hour-left-in-the-studio throwaway jobs. Booker T. and the MGs had been in town in late '65 with the Stax revue for a show, and I had booked them to help me with some studio themes. Booker T.'s sax player was Packy Axton, whose mom, Estelle Axton, co-owned Stax. We finished the jingles and then, just for fun, I started beating on my conga drum: one, two, bop-bop. I'd read it was what slaves used as a code beat, a warning at secret meetings that massa was coming; the change-up of rhythm was the signal to start their emotional dances and laughter, to fool massa that they were happy and contented. I was one-twoing and shouted out a chord to Booker T. to play on the piano. The rest of the band fell in and found there was plenty of room to work within the open confines of my rhythm. It was (forgive me) edgier, or maybe jazzier, than the standard R&B instrumental. The next day I came by this little studio to pick up the tapes of the jingles to mix them down from eight tracks to stereo. In the process I listened to that instrumental, and something told me that I had a hit . . . but I had to add something.

So I called the owner of a record shop in Santa Monica, a friend of mine, and said: "Look, I need your daughter and maybe three friends to do a handclap for me and some 'Yeah, yeahs' in an amen-corner style." I set up the mikes and told 'em I wanted the background feel of a little party, a live feel, some exhortation in back of the music. It took an hour, and I paid them, and for three or four days I'd come in and mix it. By the fourth day I had it, but I didn't know what to call it. Then I looked around this old dump of a studio, which I was using because it was cheap, and I saw a hole in the wall. Good enough. The next morning was "Soul Time" on KGFJ, and out came "Hole in the Wall" by the Packers. The listeners caught the groove right away. I put the single out on Pure Soul, another of my record labels, and it raced to the top of the national R&B charts and became a million seller.

I was always buying and selling masters, looking for material I could put out or make a profit on by selling it to someone else. Ray Charles wanted to buy one of my masters once, and I went up to his office and found him sitting at the control board. We throw the tape on, and he listens and says, "Well, I got do some mixing, bring up the horns here, bring up the drums here—"

I say, "Wait a minute; you can't see."

"Montague," he says, and his voice gets impatient because he must have had this conversation a thousand times before, "*I'm* gonna mix this." And he proceeded to take apart the song and put it back together, moving his fingers from knob to knob. A couple of times I challenged what he heard, and then I realized he was right and had to back down. Another time he heard a violin that was out of tune and mixed it down, all part of what a producer does whenever you engineer a record from multitrack down to stereo. Man, my ego was at stake here; I was a pretty good producer, and I'd already listened to it and liked it. Now Ray said he was going to correct another problem by splicing out a small section. He took out a razor blade.

"Ray, I know you been lyin' to everybody," I said. I didn't think he could do it. "Ray, you may cut yourself." He cued up the tape. "Ray, I'm good. I know I can splice."

"Montague," he said, "I will splice the *a* out of *ass*." And there wasn't anything left for me to say. Just another reason why they call him the Genius.

I got a call around this time from a guy in New York who wanted to set up a record company, asking me if I could locate some old Vee Jay masters he could buy. I had a friend, Danny Selvin, who owned a bunch, and we negotiated a price, $1,000 per master. Catch the next plane out, the businessman said. We met in East Orange, New Jersey, where it became apparent that this was a mob guy trying to break into a new business. He had a couple associates in fur-lined coats come in with $50 and $100 bills in shopping bags. They counted out the money for Danny, and we gave him the masters. Now, I had my own fee coming for doing this deal, but the businessman had decided he was going to test me. He'd asked Danny privately whether Danny was giving me a kickback; it apparently bothered him that I might be double-dipping. Suddenly, he pulls a gun on me and asks me about it.

I fly off the handle. "You son of a bitch!" I shout. "Who do you think you are?" Maybe I was taking myself too seriously, but my position in life was that nobody ever screwed around with Magnificent Montague, so gun or no gun, I charge the guy. "You can't fuck with me like that—I came out here to set up a business for you!" He looks at me and says, "You ain't nothing but a crazy ghetto motherfucker!" Call me guilty of bad judgment but hey, I got paid.

There were so many things I wanted to do—so many records I wanted to produce, masters I wanted to buy, historical items I wanted to collect; a recording studio I wanted to build; a radio station I still dreamed of starting—that deejaying became a burden. Oh, I loved performing for an audience, but it takes its toll. By 1967

I was looking forty straight in the eye, and I decided I'd had enough. I'd been on the air nearly fifteen straight years, been in every city I could imagine, and the business was changing. Stations were learning how to format themselves to squeeze in more music and more commercials, and that didn't leave much room for the deejay. The writing was on the wall. I wasn't about to have anybody tell me what to do, how to perform, ever. I said good-bye to KGFJ and my darlings in April, throwing a farewell concert at the Shrine Auditorium, emceed by the fabulously foul-mouthed Rudy Ray Moore. Onto the stage, one after another, careened a group of soul shouters that would have made a great radio programming lineup any day of the week: Solomon Burke, the Packers, Lowell Fulsom, Jimmy Reed, Little Richard, Dyke and the Blazers, Gene Chandler, Hugh Masekela, Mary Love, John Lee Hooker, Bob and Earl—and a dozen more. "Montague Will Burn No More," declared a large headline in Los Angeles's black newspaper, the *Sentinel*.

They were wrong. I just wasn't going to burn in public. I spent the next two years recording a series of spoken-word albums that were, in my mind, the best response to the rebellion I had just lived through. I saw a market void that I could fill, but I also saw an intellectual void. I felt I was way ahead of the new black-studies movement that was causing unrest on college campuses. So I put out a five-album package about the role of the black man. The individual records highlighted the Buffalo Soldiers, a then little-known Negro regiment; memorable passages by Dr. King (the record came out just after his murder in Memphis); various blacks who had played decisive roles but were ignored by history; the philosophy of James Baldwin, read by the man himself; and the poetry of Langston Hughes, also read by the author. I called it my Black America series and sold it to one of the nation's leading manufacturers of school audio-visual equipment.

I went back to my tape recordings of Malcolm X's street-corner speeches and put out *The Un-stilled Voice of Malcolm X*. I recorded my own poetry as an album, *Soul Poems for Soul People*. I went back to church by recording an album of essays combining my readings of biblical verse and gospel music to explore the stories of people like Moses, Isaiah, and Matthew. I called it *Who Wrote the Bible?* I dug out my story of Henry J. that I'd written in New York and had some copies made.

And I wanted to make a personal statement on the turmoil that was surrounding us, so I cut a single called "I Too Am an American," which sold about 50,000 copies in a tense Los Angeles:

> *I too am an American*
> *Black as the night that surrounds me*
> *Here I was born, and here I'll stay*
> *I have seen the human drama*
> *I believe in God, who made of one blood all nations on earth . . .*
> *But most of all I believe in patience*
> *Patience with the weakness of the weak and the strength of the strong*
> *And the prejudice of the ignorant and the ignorance of the blind*
> *And above all, patience with my country . . .*
> *I too am an American*
> *I've been slaved, but so have you*
> *Refused, abused and used, but so have you*
> *Yet there is something in human nature which always makes people*
> *Give merit to anyone, no matter what the color of their skin . . .*

Around this time my old friend Tom Bradley was trying to make a similar statement that would have seemed audacious—no, I'll make it plainer: crazy—while Los Angeles was burning. He had won election to the Los Angeles City Council in 1963, the first Negro ever elected. (His victory came a few months after another Negro was appointed to fill a council vacancy.) As 1969 approached, he declared his candidacy for mayor against the incumbent, my old nemesis, Sam Yorty, who'd already served two terms. I saw this in the starkest terms of good versus evil, a straight-shooting black ex-cop against an old white man who'd done his best to make me look like some sort of evil genie during the riots. I was glad to emcee some of Tom's campaign events. But Los Angeles does not have a large black population—never more than perhaps 15 percent and only 10 percent these days—and as decent a man as Tom was, his city was dominated by whites who not only were wary of social change but had just gone through the 1968 presidential campaign, when both George Wallace and Richard Nixon beat the country over the head with their "law-and-order" theme.

I'll tell you what Los Angeles was like then. There's a Jewish deli in Beverly Hills that everybody knows, Nate 'n Al's. Screenwriters love to eat there, people like that. It's near Bel Air, where I bought a beautiful home on Roscomare Road in 1966 in a previously all-white neighborhood with show-business types such as Alfred Hitchcock and Elizabeth Taylor's mother. My son, Martin, was practically raised at Nate 'n Al's, we ate there so often. But whenever we went in there, the three of us, we would get the looks that interracial families always got—still get. Some of the women would ask Rose, when I wasn't there: "Darling, how does it feel to be married to the *schwarzer?*" They thought Rose was a Jew because of her last name, Catalon. They'd ask the owner of the restaurant, Mrs. Mendelson, "What *is* she?" She'd reply: "What do you *want* her to be?" I told Mrs. Mendelson one day that I was part Jewish, so she'd tell the women: "Oh, he's half *schwarzer* and half Jew." My son would go into the kitchen, because some of the cooks were French Jews from Africa, and Martin had learned some of the language from Rose. In the restaurant people would invite my son to their table but not say a damned word to me. They'd say hello to Rose, but it was like I didn't exist. That was Los Angeles in the sixties. Tom Bradley, who was as black as me, never had a chance, even against a lame, awkward incumbent, even with the support of rich West Los Angeles liberals. Tom beat Yorty easily when they were part of a large field in the general election in early 1969, but when the two met in a runoff that spring, it was different. If you thought Johnnie Cochran played the race card in the O. J. Simpson trial, it was nothing compared to what Sam Yorty did to Tom Bradley when they went one on one. He tried to make Tom—the most moderate of blacks, an ex-UCLA track star, ex-cop, and attorney—look like a member of the Black Panthers. Elect Tom and white cops would

quit the force, and then nobody would be safe from the black
hordes, he said. Mayor Yorty positioned himself as the guardian of
civilization and Tom as the leader of a mob, and he won reelection.
Even in defeat, though, we felt a sense of progress and hope.

Going off the air meant that, for the first time since I ran away
from home, I was committed to settling down in one spot. That
liberated Rose, who'd been forced to drop out of high school when
I stole her away from Lafayette, and it gave Martin, who'd been
forced to change schools every couple years, a chance for some sta-
bility. Rose wanted to get her high school diploma and a whole lot
more. She took night classes at a local high school, transferred to
Santa Monica Community College, and then went to UCLA. She
fell in love with history and eventually got her bachelor's degree
in that subject—and began schooling me.

Virtually all of what I'd collected to this point was books. Thousands of 'em. But the more Rose studied, the more names she
heard, the more periods she became familiar with, and the more
she influenced me to broaden my range. I began to buy paintings
and to understand their significance. She got me interested in
ephemera like greeting cards, children's toys, and magazine covers from another century, all of them lessons in the brutally racist
way blacks were caricatured—but each of them honest documen-
tation of what the past, good or bad, had felt like. Within a couple
of years in the seventies I was poking around for rare movie posters of all-black films and then for the prints themselves. I was running down all the artwork used to sell Cream of Wheat, Niggerhead
Tobacco, Uncle Ben's Molasses, Korn Kink Malted Corn Flakes—
here, check out the 1907 magazine ad for Korn Kink showing a
kinky-haired Negro boy and asking: "Ain't he a likely pickanniny?
That's what comes from eatin' co'n. Co'n fed folks is cheerful. They
is always up an' doin'. You've no idea how much good eatin' they
is in a package of Ko'n Kinks until you try it. It's good for the fambly
and for every one of the fambly."

Now, blacks—and whites—might be embarrassed by this, but
the truth was that these faces were popular with whites because so

many middle-class Americans had black domestic help (what other jobs were we allowed to have?) and they trusted blacks with the most essential of household duties and products. It went back to slavery. Of course, when the gas stove finally replaced the old wood stove, you began to see all the ads change—little white ladies with white aprons, no dirt, no soot, no need for blacks to do the work. When television began, it was a different ball game. You could no longer exaggerate features of blacks to make whites feel safer; you had to show actual human images, and rather than do that, TV made us invisible again. But that was the glorious thing about what our history collection, as it burgeoned, was teaching us—we had not *always* been invisible.

Rose became fascinated with advertising. She learned, for example, that Uncle Ben's rice grew out of science: there was this black farmer in Texas who kept winning a state rice-growing contest, and after he died in the forties, a couple of white men with money came along and decided to market his formula. They met at a restaurant to talk business, saw the black doorman, and said: "That's the face!" He became Uncle Ben.

Rose was the one who began framing my pictures and matting the lithographs. Rose was the one who finally got sick of stumbling into boxes and let me decorate our Bel Air home with the collection, so that the paintings and drawings and framed artifacts jumped out at you when you walked in the door. Bam! A framed *Collier's* magazine cover from the twenties showing a little white boy applying white paint to a black friend's face, pure innocence. Bam! *The African,* a stunning mid-nineteenth-century work by Rudolf von Mehoffer, a portrait painter of German royalty. Bam! My priceless pastel-made-from-peanut-oils flower painting by George Washington Carver that I'd bought from the stepdaughter of one of Dr. Carver's young white Southern assistants. Bam! Scores of Cream of Wheat posters. (I might have gone a little too far; I enclosed a balcony so I had more exhibit room. Belated apology, Rose darling.)

Rose was the one who began pointing me toward secondary source materials in the form of white publications that had taken early notice of black achievement. This meant that if I walked into a store and saw a pile of old theater magazines, I'd go through every page looking for an article about somebody black. It's a pain in the butt but it brings you things like a 1903 article from a mainstream magazine called *The Theater* favorably recounting a play called *In Dahomey,* the first Negro-written, Negro-performed play on Broadway, with music by the immortal composer Will Marion Cook and starring Bert Williams. The play included a hilarious scene in which a medicine man promises to turn all colored people white. "The unquestionable success of this enterprise is likely to result in renewed and more ambitious efforts in this direction," the magazine wrote. "Bert Williams has long enjoyed the reputation of being a vastly funnier man than any white comedian now on the American stage." (A picture caption notes that "Mr. Williams is not really as black as he is painted here, being compelled to 'cork up' for stage purposes owing to his light complexion.")

The secondary materials we acquired included countless art indexes and led to one of my most intriguing finds. I was at a National Association of Broadcasters convention in New Orleans when I read about an estate sale at a high-tone art dealership in the French Quarter. Wandering in, I noticed a painting with a young black man in it. The scene was a young woman preparing for a masked ball, her servant seeming deliciously bored by her vanity. The price was beyond my beyond, but I telephoned Rose and asked her what we knew about the artist, Jean-Pierre Vallet, and then went back and told the salesman I'd be back the next day. At home Rose kept digging. By the time we talked again that night she was able to tell me that *Before the Masked Ball,* as the painting is known, was painted around 1865 and had been a gift from Queen Wilhemina of Holland to Kaiser Wilhelm's daughter, Beatrix. (We later learned that Beatrix had sold the painting to Colonel and Mrs. Bluford H. J. Balter and that it had hung for the previous seventy years in the Blufords' Mississippi beach mansion until the couple's deaths.) But more important was what our art encyclopedias told us: Vallet was a student of Jean-Auguste Ingres, and only three of

Vallet's works were known to exist in the world. I didn't know Vallet from the Valentinos, but I had to have this. I wrote my check and they shipped it home . . . and then the real fun started. A few weeks later I got a call from that New Orleans art house asking if I'd be willing to part with the painting at a substantial profit; it seemed another buyer had come along after I left offering significantly more. I politely told them no. *Before the Masked Ball* has ever since been displayed in a prominent position in my house. It's one of my favorites.

I finally built my studio on Vermont at 84th in the heart of South-Central L.A. using what I'd learned at the hands of Don Robey in Houston and Jimmy and Vivian Bracken at Vee Jay in Chicago. I was convinced I could tap into a wealth of undiscovered black talent that didn't know where to go for an audition and had no access to the equipment needed to make a demo. Bobby Womack, who'd started with Sam Cooke's SAR label, recorded for me. So did a group called the Watts 103d Street Band and the Romeos. In the early seventies those two bands merged to become War, which later recorded with the British star Eric Burdon. I was hoping to lure Hollywood record companies to use my studio, but the truth was they just didn't feel comfortable coming to the 'hood.

Around this time Berry Gordy moved Motown to Los Angeles and offered me a position as special assistant to the president. He needed somebody to work the deejays and advise him on promotion and marketing, because Motown was beginning to lose its advantage; you could almost chart it from the day Doctor King was assassinated in '68. Black music quickly began to surrender its melodic core to the service of rhythm, a funkier rhythm, a fiercer rhythm, one bent on making a statement of independence. This change contradicted the blander way Motown had been producing itself, and there was nothing Berry could do about it. He had enjoyed a window of only a few years—maybe 1963 to 1966, to be arbitrary—in which there was a rough consensus between young blacks and whites, an unverbalized understanding of what America might be, of what was right and wrong. It could not last.

When Berry married off his daughter, Hazel, to Jermaine Jackson of the Jackson Five in 1972, he threw a spectacular half-million-dollar wedding reception at the Beverly Hills Hotel. I saw him talking to Rose, and the next thing I knew, it had been agreed that the newlyweds would continue the reception at our home. Gordy put his arms around them and approached me with that warm smile. "Magnificent, they need some culture. Now's the time. Do you mind?"

"Do I mind? You already wooed Rose. I'm just the curator."

Gordy wanted Hazel, whom I'd known since her childhood in Detroit, and Jermaine to sample my collection. With an *Ebony* magazine photographer in tow, we spent the next couple hours on a minitour. It was one of those times—not the first time—that I thought wistfully about what it would be like to have the collection in a real museum, instead of keeping most of it in a warehouse thirty miles away. But it was just a dream. There was too much to do. I was doing well enough now to send Rose and Martin on two trips to Europe within three years. Martin had already learned French from both Rose and Le Lycée Français de Los Angeles, the private academy he attended.

Around the same time I got a surprise: an offer to go back on the air in the biggest market yet without leaving Los Angeles. XPRS was one of the legendary "border radio" stations, broadcasting 100,000 watts out of Tijuana and hitting fifteen states. They'd hired a whole crew, including Wolfman Jack, the famed L.A. oldies deejay Art Laboe, and another L.A. legend, "Emperor Bob" Hudson. Wolfman wasn't there long, because George Lucas had cast him as the mostly unseen radio voice in *American Graffiti,* which was just about to come out. Up till that time Wolfman had kept his face a secret, so nobody would know he was white. But fame tempted him. (It was worth it. For the next ten years Wolfman hosted a network TV rock 'n' roll show, looking his white self while still talking black. But God got even. Wolfman had just put out his autobiography in 1995 and was planning his promotional tour when, at only fifty-seven, he died of a heart attack at his home in North Carolina.)

Of course, I was fooling my listeners, too. From the way the station promoted itself, they thought Montague was back on the air in Mexico, broadcasting live, when Montague was actually going to a studio in Los Angeles every day, doing a three-hour taped R&B show and handing the tape to a courier, who took it down south to be broadcast the next day.

The next artist I took a liking to seems like a logical progression, but only in hindsight. Soul had come on stronger than ever, big and brash and melodic, and then funk came aboard and emphasized the rhythm—even more direct, in your face. A couple years of that and people want to swing the pendulum the other way, make it mellow, ease it a little. The man who showed up in 1973 to take them there was getting too old, at twenty-nine, to be a nobody. He'd been a kid piano player, cut a couple records as a solo artist under a different name in the early sixties, and then, like so many people who can't make it at the microphone, found another way into the business, as an artist-and-repertoire man. Then in '69 he'd taken another crack, forming a girl trio called Love Unlimited and becoming the leader of his own forty-piece band, the Love Unlimited Orchestra. He put his own deep, deep, *deep* voice over all those strings and did something that struck a chord with me: he dedicated every inch of his performance to *his* darlings. Every song was direct from him to the ladies: "Take it off, baby, take it all off. . . . I want you the way you came into the world. . . . I don't want to see no panties. . . . Take off that brassiere, my dear." And because of how fast the culture had changed sexually in just the last few years—people in their thirties had seen how much fun the kids were having, and realized that they'd missed out, that they'd better make their move now—Barry White touched a nerve he'd never been able to touch before.

I met Barry, and I liked him—a huge fellow, so big people used to mock him as the Love Walrus—and I knew his first single, "I'm Gonna Love You Just a Little Bit More, Baby," was going to be a hit, but I told his record company that they couldn't get it on KGFJ or the Top-40 stations because of the way they did business in those days. They wouldn't play it until it was on the charts—until some other station made it a hit. So with the understanding that there'd be a payback, I jumped on the record on my XPRS show, playing it every fifteen minutes (it was a perfect fit, my poetry introducing Barry's), sending a team of runners to record shops in San Diego and other cities to give away hundreds of copies, trying to create a buzz, a demand. It worked. In six weeks his hypnotic, elaborate record hit the charts; he was a phenomenon, the forerunner of disco—the forerunner, if you will, of rap, presenting himself more by speaking his lyrics than singing them, charting five number-one R&B hits and seven other Top-10 R&B hits in the next six years—five of which also wound up in the Top-10 pop charts. God knows the man had a lot of fun poked at him, and God knows he had a long dry spell in the eighties, but he pulled out of it. Quincy Jones used him on a single in '89, and Barry started touring everywhere from Lebanon to Kenya to Brazil and became a cult figure on one of those Fox TV shows about yuppie lawyers . . . still pulling in his darlings.

My own darlings, meanwhile, were going to gather for a Montague tribute concert that the San Diego Elks Club was throwing right as I was trying to break Barry. His record company was more than happy to give him to me to headline the show. It was a great feeling, being out in public again, having a little bit of the limelight again. But you know me. It couldn't last. Four weeks later, I got fired. And it was all Tom Bradley's fault.

Well, make that Sam Yorty's fault.

Here we were, in '73, and Los Angeles was having another mayoral election. Tom was determined to unseat Sam, and this time his odds looked good. He'd remained a dignified presence on the City Council, while Sam had made an ass of himself by running for president in the Republican primaries in 1972—right as the Republican incumbent, Nixon, campaigned for reelection! (Once again, the *Los Angeles Times*'s political cartoonist put it best: Conrad drew a picture of a "Yorty for President" sign on a tree and captioned it "The sap is running in the snows of New Hampshire.") I felt Tom's campaign gaining fire as I introduced him from one neighborhood

rally to another, just as I'd done in '69, and as election day neared
it seemed logical for me to share my feelings with my XPRS audience, even though many of them lived outside L.A.

XPRS terminated me the day after my "unauthorized endorse-
ment" aired. It was worth it: Tom creamed Yorty 56 percent to 34
percent. Do you know what that meant in a city that hadn't had
an integrated fire department until '55 or fully integrated police
cars until '62? It was one of the most promising days in American
racial history, and maybe in retrospect it was one of the last promising ones.

I went back to my studio, back to other projects. I had a friend
in the record business who used to comanage Bob Dylan for the
William Morris Agency. He was out of work and wanted to go into
business, and he asked me to help him with his proposal. He was
going to set up a shop on Sunset Boulevard selling only chocolate
chip cookies. He had six varieties, and he was going to focus on the
entertainment industry. "The chocolate chip cookie is the superstar of cookies," the proposal read. "I make a truly exceptional
chocolate chip cookie. . . . if the idea catches on in Los Angeles,
other shops could be opened." He estimated spending about sixty
thousand dollars a year and making a profit of thirty thousand.
"Not until 1970, when Wally Amos started to bake his secret recipe,
has any chocolate chip cookie been so thoroughly authentic and
delicious," boasted the proposal. Famous Amos backed that up.

In 1976 I was asked to speak on a panel at a national broadcasting convention in Washington, and it rekindled that dream of
building my own station. But having a dream rekindled is miles
away from knowing how to get it. Nothing in my life around turntables and microphones had prepared me for something as sophisticated as that. And nothing in my life had made enough money
to hire the battery of lawyers and other experts needed to pull it off.
I was about to plunge into the hardest years of my life, and one of
the most wearying yarns about man versus government (with brief
refrains on man versus endangered species, man versus heat ex-
haustion, and man versus tractor driving) that you ever heard.

11 The Climb

I couldn't buy somebody else's radio station. That would cost millions, and the biggest budget I could scrape together was only about three hundred thousand. I'd have to build my own. I gave myself three years to do it. I knew that the federal government controlled the number of stations, but to my embarrassment that was all I knew. The first snatch of jargon I heard was "construction permit." Where did I get one?

I'd hired a communications attorney in Washington, but he charged two hundred fifty dollars an hour, and I needed to limit his time. We'd just sold our house and moved to an apartment off Wilshire Boulevard near UCLA, where Rose had gone back to school and where I did a daily workout at the track. "Montague," she said, "why don't you go over to UCLA and monitor the Communications Department classes, learn something about this?"

So I started going up to the communications law library, and I got lucky. I met this professor named Wexler who was a do-gooder, a man who liked to fight the government on the people's behalf— and he turned out to have been a KGFJ listener. Could I sit in on his classes? "Yes," he said, "but only if you do a lecture on programming first."

For a year I haunted the Communications Department, studying the books for every case I could find that came before the FCC. I started reading *Broadcasting* magazine, which I never knew existed. The more I read, the clearer it got that blacks simply did not do this. The government hadn't awarded a black man a construction permit for a radio station since a pair of Detroit physicians started WCHB in Detroit in the fifties—and it took most of a decade between the time they got the permit and turned on the station. A black man building a radio station in a predominantly white market was unheard of, but that wasn't why I was doing it. I was a businessman, and business had no color to me. I would not be bound by anybody's racial box.

I had no clue about the inner workings of the transmitter or the antenna—the "stick." I didn't know who to ask. I had never learned about different hardware manufacturers—one makes the antenna, one makes the tower, one makes the oscillator. I didn't know the difference between a maintenance engineer and chief engineer. (I used to think being banned from the studio because of segregation in Texas had been a blessing because it forced me to understand my audience better by doing all those remote broadcasts; now I realized the cost.) I was going to wind up building an FM station somewhere, simply because there were more frequencies available, but I didn't know much about the FM side of the dial; I had never worked on it. When I was on the air, nobody wanted FM frequencies; you could build an FM station in the old days for a few thousand dollars. But in the sixties the government authorized stereo broadcasting, and the market exploded.

I called a couple of white ex-jockeys I knew who'd gone into sales and then built a little station, and they agreed to hip me. They

loaned me some books. The regulations said anybody could get a
construction permit as long as he was a citizen, had no felonies, and
had the money and the technical qualifications—but first the FCC
had to create a new channel, space on the dial for another frequency.

The president at the time, Jimmy Carter, gave me a break, too.
I found out that his administration had appointed the first black
FCC commissioner, Benjamin Hooks, and that the agency was taking steps to open the airwaves, to create thousands more channels—and more importantly, was making it easier for the little guy.
It used to be that you would have to go out and search with an engineer to figure out whether you could, say, create an FM station
broadcasting at frequency 101.8 in village X. You'd pay for the study
and submit it to the FCC, and then the government engineers
would determine whether you were right. But now, to help entre-
preneurs who couldn't afford that gamble, the FCC was going to
publish a list of available new channels and their classifications.

How did I know about this change? Because by now on my
daily trips to UCLA, which had become the equivalent of a full-
time job, I was reading the *Federal Register,* which contains every
regulatory change the federal bureaucracy makes every day.

Now, none of these new channels could be put in major cities;
those places were already saturated. You had to get on the outskirts
and come in with your signal, turn your antenna a certain way to
expand your reach. Rose and I were going to go anywhere in Southern California we had to go, cow town or no cow town. And then
one day I saw a listing in the *Federal Register:* class B frequency,
50,000 watts, Palm Springs. We'd been going down to Palm
Springs many weekends with our son and always talked about living down there and running a little station. It was one of the rich-
est resort areas in the world, a natural.

We'd spend the next six years pulling our hair out before anybody heard the first song through a radio on that new frequency,
106 FM.

First, I had to hire an engineer to show the FCC that we could
make this frequency work. The FCC gives you a three-mile area to

find a place to put the stick. You cannot go outside those coordinates. I couldn't read a topographical map, so I found an engineering firm—southern crackers, but this was business—that priced it out for me. I had to do more than just tell the FCC where I'd put the stick, though. I also had to prove I had financing—prove I had the ability to buy the land—and draw up an annual profit-and-loss statement.

And I had to do it better than all the other people who wanted this same valuable frequency. Because building a radio station is a competitive, cutthroat battle to the death.

We wouldn't know how many other parties we had to fight until all the applications were tendered in Washington a few months later. Then everything would go on public display, and all the competitors would start looking for ways to poke holes in their opponents' plans. Back then, the FCC only checked applications for minimal compliance; it assumed the combatants would find flaws in their rivals that would allow the agency to award the construction permit to the best applicant. There were certain things you could have going for you. If you had broadcast experience, that was good. If you already owned a broadcasting facility, that was bad.

As we put the application together—always listing Rose as the president and general manager, because she was the one with the best business sense—we had to find a bank to give us credit, get quotes from equipment companies, and find some land in the area the FCC had designated, about ten miles east of Palm Springs in a barren stretch of the Coachella Valley. My engineers took out that topo map and drew five places I could put the stick. "We gotta go up 3,000 feet," they told me. How do we do that? We sure couldn't drive up there to check it out. No roads. I had to hire a helicopter to fly me around the top of the terrain, and we saw a spot they said was good. Now, who owned it? Check the Riverside county recorder's office, they said. So I made my way there, trying to decipher the language of sections and coordinates, having no choice but to do this myself, aware that our money was already draining away too fast. I'd go home at night and tell Rose how lost I felt. Out of desperation, I decided to simply look for a sympathetic face in the recorder's office, and finally somebody led me to somebody else who led me to one of the trained map readers. The map reader took pity on me and showed me that the land I wanted was owned by Southern Pacific. They own all the land out there for twenty miles. We cut a lease arrangement, and now we could finally file the damn application. And now, like roller derby, all the applicants began trying to knock the others down, finding some relevant fact that would downgrade the opponents.

This went on for two or three years. I had thousands of pages of FCC proceedings. There were six of us in the running, and finally, after we'd beaten each other up for a long time, four of the applicants got tired or saw the writing on the wall and took themselves out. Now it was just me and a guy who owned a station in Las Vegas—a small advantage to me, but not critical. You're looking for a document he didn't sign, a budget claim that contradicts his costs—anything. Everything goes to the offices of the FCC's Broadcast Bureau, and they determine whether it's a relevant issue for an FCC administrative law judge to consider. But first you go to interrogatories, kind of like discovery in a court of law. That's where your legal bills start running heavy, and you get questions like this: "Well, Mister Montague, on the application it says your name is Montague. Is that right?" Or, "Miss Catalon, what will your format be? Or is Mister Montague behind that?"

When only two applicants are left, the FCC allows you to merge, but that wasn't going to happen here after all that fighting and hating. This ain't for no fainthearted son of a bitch. And it's why so few blacks ever got a piece of the action—maybe 2 percent of the five thousand stations that were on the air when I started my push had even a share of black ownership. In depositions I was so rough on my opponent that he told my lawyer one day, "Mister Montague sits there and looks at me like he hates me, like he could kill me." He was trying to show that he was using blacks in his partnership, but we exposed him by showing he'd brought in one black and given him precisely 1 percent participation, pure tokenism. His side came back on me: "How do you make your money, Mister Montague?" I had so many irons in the fire that it was difficult to answer. And all the while, my attorney's meter was going click, click, click.

I was getting antsy. I had to knock this guy out, so I put a detective on him. I was looking for dirt, financial or personal, because character counted as well as financial plan. His antenna site was on another hill maybe a half-mile from mine, and one day I was in the desert talking to an old-timer who lived in a lean-to, somebody who sounded like he knew every inch of the place. We were talking about an easement problem I had, and he took me around the side of the mountain and mentioned something he'd heard from one of the rangers: my opponent's land was on the edge of an endangered wildlife refuge.

Up to that moment I had never cared about the environment, especially the occupants of it who crawled. But it turned out that under the federal Endangered Species Act, only a few years old at the time, something called the fringe-toed lizard had been declared a protected species by the Environmental Protection Agency—and packs of them liked to slither in and out of these sandy, grass-dotted hills. You couldn't disturb the ground in the wildlife refuge.

You know how oblivious government agencies are to one another. The FCC didn't know the EPA's rules. It was my civic obligation to tell them. In retrospect, it was the knockout punch to my opponent's application. I thought I'd weakened him enough now to offer a deal: I would buy him out for the amount of money he'd spent so far. It took five months before the FCC approved that, but finally I had my construction permit. I walked up and down Wilshire Boulevard saying to myself: Oh, God, I did it! It's a dream come true! I had my marketing and programming plans ready to go.

But my troubles were just beginning, because now I had to build the sucker.

For one thing, my costs were out of control. This had taken so much longer than I anticipated, and inflation was so rampant in the late seventies, that I needed to borrow a couple hundred thousand dollars more to make this work. Every cent I had, and many cents I didn't have, were tied up in this.

I didn't have two basic things on my antenna site: electricity or a road. The only access to the top was on the other side of the mountain, and we were so far from civilization that there were no power lines in sight—a factor we had neglected to include in our budget. The power company, which was primarily an irrigation district, didn't want to deal with us because the cost was prohibitive. I needed another guide. I started talking to one of the officials of this little power company and wound up breaking bread with him—wound up becoming his son's godfather. Okay, he said, it can be done, but I would have to put it on paper and submit it to the board. He came back and told me the utility would do it for me if I paid the hundred-thousand-dollar cost, and only after I built the service roads—one going up and the other coming down.

But first that fringe-toed lizard up and nearly bit me in the ass.

To get to my hill, I had to cut an access road across some federal property. The U.S. Bureau of Land Management knew about the endangered lizard and tried to stop me, forcing me to spend more money proving that I would narrowly miss the wildlife refuge. We then had to fight with the county government, which didn't want to issue a local building permit because the antenna would look ugly and spoil the mountainside. They left that hanging over our heads.

I paid the money for the electricity, but I didn't have the money—another $100,000—to hire a road-building company to let us get to the top of the hill. My original $300,000 budget had ballooned to $650,000. In the meantime, we were getting a number of offers from other broadcasters to buy our construction permit. A common way of making money in radio is to speculatively obtain a construction permit and then sell it. But my whole life, and Rose's too, was tied up in this. We went looking for help from influential blacks in the entertainment business, trying to sell private stock in the station, but couldn't interest them. We turned down some other offers of participation because it would have meant sharing control, and I didn't want to budge on that.

It was never my intent to build the roads myself. I was fifty-one years old, and the hardest labor I'd ever done was a ninety-minute daily workout at UCLA, where some of my ex-listeners who'd been star Bruins athletes helped put me through my paces. But one day at the county planning department I saw a young guy sitting there, a country boy who drove a tractor-trailer, and I got to talking to him about what I wanted to do. He said, "Why dontcha rent the tractors? I got a tractor company, and we'll build it." We cut a deal. It meant I was going to be riding a goddamned Caterpillar tractor and doing a whole lot more than I bargained for.

One of the things I didn't know was that you don't build a road by piling material up; you build a road by pushing the dirt down. And before we got to that point, we had to find a way to clear a path to get the Cats up the hill, 'cause there wasn't any road to begin with. All we had were these big boulders that need to be cleared. My tractor-trailer friend said his equipment wasn't cut out to do that job. What should I do? "Get a Jeep, get you some chisels, get you some workers." So I got me some migrant workers, made one who spoke English the foreman, and set up some tents where they could sleep so they could work night and day, and for three months we hammered and chiseled. We got on our knees and hammered to get those boulders out the way inch by inch so we could take those Cats up there, to 3,000 feet, to start building the road. We worked three months in 115-degree heat. Many times they threatened me. "Me no see no end!" Sure, I was out there too, 'cause otherwise they wouldn't have stayed out there, either! I got even blacker with that sun eating my ass up. I had a deal with a hotel in Palm Springs: I didn't stay there all night, but I used a room periodically to clean myself up so when I came back to L.A. nobody knew what I'd been doing.

Well, we get a third up that damned mountain and they quit on me. "We no gonna do no more. You mucho loco." I go back to John and Jesse, the two tractor-trailer guys, and they agree to bring in a different kind of tractor, but they warn me we can only do five yards at a time before we have to stop. Oh, and the snakes! Snakes for days! Big, long snakes. John would drive the tractor, inch by inch, and Jesse and I would walk alongside, hosing it down, trying to keep it from overheating.

Two weeks of this and we're halfway up when, on a day I was driving the tractor, the damn thing slid down the mountain. They figured out a way to gun the engine and get it back on track, but I was sure my time had come. Finally we were able to clear a path so that we could move all the equipment to the top and start building the road. I had no plans, nothing laid out, no survey—that saved me thirty thousand. We worked about three hours a day because that was all we could stand. The workers were half-drunk 'cause I kept them supplied with beer and food.

Finally the first road is built and it's time to start on the second road. Except before we do that, we run the test of the first road: can we drive a truck, filled with equipment, up it?

No, we cannot. We didn't make the grade low enough. Damned truck couldn't get a third of the way up, the path was so steep. More grading, more misery. But at least we got that first road, so the power people could come up and install sixty poles to provide the transmitter with electricity.

I had to buy the poles, naturally, and even then there was a catch: the winds were too high to throw the poles in a truck, so they had to be individually helicoptered in; a crew would catch 'em and anchor them down in cement. I kept reassuring myself. This is all part of my investment; it's going to be worth a couple million; it's going to be the most powerful station in Palm Springs. I'm not crazy. I'm not crazy. I'm not crazy.

Okay, now the day of reckoning comes. My engineering consultants are going to truck the equipment up to the top of the mountain, and *they* get spooked by the grade of the hill, even though we thought we had fixed it. I have to volunteer to ride with 'em. We get near the top of the hill and the truck's engine stalls. We have to get out and start shoveling dirt to make the final push. But we made it. Now the construction can start. The sixty-foot-high antenna can be erected.

And then it's time to bring up the county and federal inspectors to sign off on the project. We borrowed a utility truck, but
Rose, insisting I was too excitable, told me she'd drive everybody
up to the top. She told me to hop in the back as she started driving, but she took off before I could get in. I yelled at her to slow
down, but she was busy talking to the inspectors and didn't hear
me, so she kept going. That forced me to jog the three miles behind
her. Never mind. Once I got up there, I felt like Columbus—we
both did, proud to have done the impossible. Rose took a stick and
we attached an American flag we'd long planned to bring for this
occasion. She planted the flagstick in the ground. I looked around.
I could see all the Coachella Valley and down Interstate 10. Man, I
was on top of the world. Eventually the county planning guys
dropped their opposition to the tower's aesthetic impact.

I found a new building for my studio on Palm Canyon Drive,
Palm Spring's main drag. I fired my developer because he wanted
too much, got an architect I knew to lay the interior design out for
me, got the place wired, ran the FCC-required sixty-day test of the
signal to make sure the new frequency didn't interfere with existing ones . . . and I looked at the calendar.

It read 1983, and I wasn't even on the air.

I know what you're thinking: Montague, you gonna bring *soul*
to Palm Springs? You gonna come with the Isley Brothers?

Not a chance, my friend. I played rhythm and blues because
rhythm and blues was the only thing a black deejay was allowed
to play. I was out of the box now and into another marketplace,
and if there was one thing I knew, it was marketing and programming. I would be merely "Montague," not "Magnificent Montague," on KPLM 106 FM, and I would come not with the Isley Brothers but the Dorsey Brothers.

Years earlier Rose, two friends, and I had gone down to Palm
Springs over and over, posing as a music survey company, and
conducted a thousand interviews with people forty and older. To
my amazement, there was no station on the air there specializing
in the big band sound of the thirties and forties, the very sensibil-

ity that would connect with a huge population of people now in their sixties and seventies.

Now, I hadn't grown up with that sound. It was about ten years before my time, so I had my work cut out. All the while I was haunting the UCLA Communications Department, I was investing a little time each day at another library on campus and reading thirty-year-old back issues of *Billboard* and *Variety*. I hired a collector who helped me get my hands on thousands of records of the era, the top sellers by Glenn Miller, Count Basie, Woody Herman, Duke Ellington, Tony Bennett, Sinatra, you name it. I researched all these entertainers' bios so I could manufacture my own poetry to put behind their records; I needed the geriatric set to think I was one of them when I came on the air.

Like I said, Rose was the boss. I just wanted to be the programmer and deejay. She'd worked in an ad agency to gain experience in that side of the business. I'd be able to concentrate on captivating the audience. It wasn't going to matter that I was black. I was going to charm them so much they would believe I was one of them. No one would know whence I came. I would float down, as if from some heavenly bandstand.

Just to make sure our competitors didn't know what was going to hit them, we played all country and western songs the first week we were on the air full-time—January 1983—no announcers, just tapes with the call letters. I wanted to make sure my signal tested right, get my jingles straight, wanted to get our sales people knowing their jobs. The start of the second week, I lined up all the clergymen in town to bless the station, had the mayor show up, touched that button, and on came the big band sound.

It was a love affair with Palm Springs from the start. We fed 'em big band music, Dixieland jazz, ballads, and what I called "ballroom blues." Within weeks a columnist in the town's newspaper was calling us "the hottest thing to hit the desert since the sun." Wrote another: "Let Montague guide you into Palm Springs as it was in its movie colony days. Tune your radio to 106 FM and soon you'll hear the musical strains of Benny Goodman, Artie Shaw, and

Glenn Miller as if you were entering a different time zone. In fact, you are."

I did two daily shows, 6 to 9 A.M. and 4 to 6 P.M., and we filled a lot of the rest with taped programming. With 50,000 watts we cut a swath through a huge area of the Coachella Valley and as far south as the Mexican border. The challenge was the same: create a picture for the audience, a rich, white, and occasionally famous audience. Mix the vanilla and the chocolate. I'd take Glenn Miller and then come back with Count Basie; I'd come back with Frank Sinatra, drop in Ella Fitzgerald and Sarah Vaughn—two black women, one up-tempo jazz and the other ballad jazz—throw in the Andrews Sisters, lily-white, and then come back with the Ink Spots (everybody loved the Ink Spots—whites love 'em because they sang four-part, middle-of-the-road harmony). Mix it together with the right anecdotes, the right poetry, the right tone in my voice, that sense of wonderment and nostalgia, mix in some scores from great forties and fifties films, some old radio shows.

We did it all ourselves, me and Rose, eighteen hours a day, tightening our belts, but it was ours and we loved that. We'd been together nearly thirty years, and now we had something we'd dreamed of all that time. She was tough on me, though. She was the one making sure we could pay the bills.

"Rose, I need a new mike," I told her once.

"The old one working?"

"Barely. It's hanging from a coat hanger."

"When the hanger breaks, you can have a new one."

Gradually, though, as time wore on, I couldn't hide from the fact that KPLM lacked the excitement of my unadulterated soul radio shows. Sometimes on the air, with an up-tempo piece on the turntable, I'd be tempted to back the record up and play four more bars, and Rose would run in there and shake her finger at me. "If you get even close to doing something like that I will fire you!" she said once. Another time she called me on the poetry I was reading. "Montague, you got too soulful tonight." A hint of dialect, a touch of slang. "Do more contemporary poetry, more classic stuff. It's not a young audience. Use some Elizabeth Barrett Browning." The audience didn't seem to mind. On rare occasions we'd get a phone call with racial overtones. I saved one that the answering machine taped. "You oughta be 'shamed to have that nigger on the radio. It's just like you Jew women to have a nigger." But really, the listeners were wonderful. They appreciated our attentiveness to their era, their memories.

As much as I'd wanted to live in Palm Springs, I hadn't bargained for what it would mean to my spirit of collecting. The real goods were back in Los Angeles, where the population was, all those places I loved to haunt. Every once in a while I'd throw a tape on instead of broadcasting live, drive back to L.A., where I had the collection in storage, and sift through it, through what now numbered thousands of objects, just trying to get my mind around it, trying to figure out what to do with it, how to tell a story through it. I was torn between two dreams: my station and my collection.

And then, in the summer of '85, I got a phone call that effectively made the decision for me. It wasn't something I wanted to deal with. A white reporter at the *Los Angeles Times* tracked me down and said he wanted to do a whatever-happened-to profile about me, to be published the following month on the twentieth anniversary of the Watts riots.

I told him to go away, that I didn't want to talk about that. I knew there'd be too much to explain, that he'd never understand.

But the man wouldn't give up. He wrote me a letter and told me he used to listen to my KGFJ show as a kid, told me several flattering things about what the show had meant to him. The letter made it harder to say no—but I did, until Rose pushed me into finally saying yes. That was how I met Bob Baker.

There was a lot he didn't tell me, because reporters never let you know about themselves; they're too busy trying to sucker you into revealing parts of yourself that you'd be better off keeping hid. He didn't brag about knowing more soul music by heart than I did. He didn't tell me what it had been like being a fan of mine in an all-white high school. He didn't tell me he'd suddenly thrown away his Beatles records and started buying nothing but soul music almost as soon as he heard me. I always figured I had white listeners, lots of them, but they weren't likely to call up and dedicate a song on the "burn" line, so I usually only ran into them long after they'd grown up, and we stumbled into each other.

Bob came down to Palm Springs, and I gave him a couple hours, but I wasn't charitable about it. I liked my anonymity, my secret existence here, and I was torn between losing that and taking a chance that somebody might finally explain where the hell "Burn, baby! Burn!" came from and what the hell it meant. If you had told either of us that we'd be friends eighteen years after the interview, let alone publishing my autobiography, we'd have laughed contemptuously. ("The thing is," Bob told me a lot later, "reporters don't *make* friends with people they write stories about. We abandon them. We're like call girls. We need to develop empathy, so we pay a lot of attention to them while we're working on the story, and a lot of times they take it the wrong way and think we want to be their friend, and we wind up having to explain, 'No, this wasn't about friendship. This was about doing a story.'" Which is why I still don't trust reporters.)

The article ran on the front of the *Times*'s Metro Section, and it began this way:

> PALM SPRINGS—To his middle-aged audience, the man who calls himself Montague is a mellifluous disc jockey whose local FM radio show is devoted to '40s music . . .
>
> He delights in frequent fan letters like the one informing him that his program is now piped through the grounds of a mobile home park.
>
> His listeners could not imagine that the same voice that now introduces Bing Crosby once invented the catch phrase that inadvertently became the slogan of the Watts riot.
>
> Twenty years ago . . .

And the damnedest thing happened: hundreds of people came out of the woodwork and telephoned me at the station—everybody from Tom Bradley to old jockeys to everyday fans from my KGFJ days to people I'd just lost track of or foolishly stopped caring about. I'd always been one to tear up my roots and move, from one station to another, from one life to another, never looking back, leaving people in the dust. "The best way to explain Montague," Rose told Bob before he came down to Palm Springs, "is that when we're driving somewhere and he misses a turn, he won't turn around and go back to it. He'll keep going. He never looks back." But now I started to feel I could look back, that it was okay to feel connected to the past, to try, in my midfifties, to put my life in perspective, to separate the disappointments from the accomplishments. And the more I thought about it, the more I became determined to put my house in order.

I was going to sell the station.

I was going to use the profits to take my collection out of storage.

I was somehow going to share it with the world.

The Montague Museum of African American History sounded like a good name. I was known. I could see the museum sprouting on Wilshire Boulevard in the old Miracle Mile district of L.A., on what they called "museum row," where the county art museum and the LaBrea Tar Pits, among others, stand.

I could make the right connections. I could get it built. Look at my life. Look at everything I'd done. Hell, I'd built my own radio station! How could creating a museum be harder than that?

12 The Collection

After we sold the Palm Springs station and moved back to L.A. in 1986, I became consumed by the vision of people like you walking through the doors of the Montague Museum of African American History, a place where you would meet all the ghosts whose works and accomplishments I'd chased.

Just as my collecting began as a crude grasp for knowledge that became more refined, your journey through the museum would have refined you. You would have realized, as few do, that the story of black history we are spoon-fed each February during Black History Month is childishly simplified, reduced to the same five or ten names. We should be told about thousands of people whose documented stories are far more fascinating—more fascinating because they are fresh and new to us and because of the power you feel when you experience those stories *collectively*. That thrill was what kept me running as a collector, and I wanted you to experience it, too—not as a black American, or a white American, or a brown American, but as an American, period. Because in what other country could these stories, including the one you've been reading, have happened?

Rose and I began the first systematic evaluation of everything I had collected. At first it wasn't so much with an eye toward building a museum ourselves as simply taking stock. A friend of mine asked me flat-out, "What's gonna happen if you drop dead?" He knew the only catalog to the collection was in my head. So over the next couple of years, while I made some money in broadcast consulting work and made plans to buy another radio station, Rose and I typed hundreds of pages, breaking down the collection by time periods, subjects, historical figures, and type—books, paintings, artifacts, movies. We framed more of our pictures and put the most delicate eighteenth- and nineteenth-century books into leather bindings. We hired a videographer to make six twenty-two-minute tapes in which I took the viewer on a guided tour. By now it was clear to outsiders that we had something special. "It isn't just a museum collection," said one of the L.A. dealers who saw the items. "It's a reference library. It's greater than any public collection of its type." All I knew was that I didn't want it in storage anymore. I wanted it seen. I figured I would find a corporation that wanted to display it. Some company would essentially buy the collection from me for a couple million and sponsor its display across the country.

Just walking into my living room, an outsider would be stunned by the paintings on the walls. Everywhere you turned, there was another ghost looking you in the face. Every repairman, tax accountant—you name it, they'd walk in, look around in astonishment, and ask, "What the hell *is* this?" And then I'd start telling them about the collection, and their race wouldn't matter, and their age wouldn't matter, and their education wouldn't matter—they would simply be turned on by the notion that somebody had accumulated all this hidden treasure, all this hidden past that nobody had told *them* about, either.

I badgered Bob Baker into writing a story about my collection for the *Los Angeles Times*. I figured that would draw the corporate offers, but it turned out that I was expected to be noble. I wasn't supposed to want to get paid for my work. The more I campaigned to find a friendly corporation, the more I kept getting steered to museums, where I was expected to donate the collection. Trouble was, if I did that, I was going to have an impoverished retirement. You don't get much Social Security when you make most of your living as an entrepreneuer. A couple years down the road, a *New York Times* writer got interested in the collection, and her paper published a spread similar to Bob's. I thought that would jump-start me, but I was wrong again.

The more frustrated I got, the more it began to dawn on me that I should stop waiting for a handout. Damn it, I had assembled, intentionally or otherwise, the premier expression of the relationship between black people and the United States. I would build my own museum.

Rose and I incorporated in 1992 as the Foundation for Preservation of African American History and set off trying to shake the money tree, particularly the branch of black entertainment magnates. But practically nothing was shaking. We came armed with an elaborate color brochure that presented the vision of the museum, but my entreaties to high-level blacks in the entertainment business were either rebuffed or ignored. Was I fooling myself? Was I doing something wrong? I lost years of sleep asking myself those questions—I still lose sleep. Was it because rich blacks in the entertainment industry didn't read? Why wasn't I connecting? Why didn't we have what the Jews have, that love of history, that commitment? I kept remembering one piece of friendly advice from a black entertainer who turned me down: "This is great, Montague, but you better get some Jews to help you." That stung. I didn't want to have to get bailed out by the Jews again. This was an endeavor that I assumed blacks would support, especially in Los Angeles, especially when it was being built by a fellow entertainer, especially when the variety of the collection touched the soul so deeply and so entertainingly.

In 1996 I rented some first-floor office space on Wilshire, in the middle of the museum district. We set up a small replica of the museum, maybe 5 percent of the collection, and invited as many black entertainers as we could think of. Only one showed up, the former pro football player, actor, and artist Bernie Casey. What had happened to my race? Why had they thrown all this away? Why had they thrown away their spirituals and their dialect poetry and all the inspirational lessons of the hard times, all the testaments to our race's strength? Why had they thrown away their culture—their American culture? Why were they calling themselves African Americans when Africa had so little to do with who they really were? Were they uncomfortable about our American history? Would they prefer to leap directly from seventeenth-century Africa to late-twentieth-century America and forget the pain in between? How could they feel demeaned by the truth? I understood that ours is an often uncomfortable history, filled with so much oppression. It bothers, or embarrasses, some blacks to acknowledge facts—like the fact that when early blacks were unable to pronounce *that,* they instead said *dat.* But that is a piece of our culture! That was who we *were!* That is history! History isn't good or bad—it simply *is.* Why were these modern blacks disconnecting their culture from that history?

I hate giving up. I hate giving in. I hate losing. But I did. In 1998 Rose and I moved to Las Vegas (we missed the desert) and transferred the collection to another storage warehouse near our new home. As we complete the writing of this book, we have spent nearly five years—both of us, virtually every day—on more microscopically cataloging it, typing summaries of each piece, and having photographs made of each item. We're exhausted and sometimes overwhelmed, but we're also nearly finished. Soon we will exhibit and sell the collection in New York to a buyer who will keep it under one roof. This became a matter of financial responsibility: I need to make sure that Rose, ten years my junior, will be taken care of when I eventually pass.

My darlings, this wasn't the ending I planned on when I began to chronicle my journey. This book and my museum, I fantasized, would come to flower simultaneously. I so wished that you could meet all the ghosts, meet them all at once, meet them all in a single day, see the cumulative effect they worked upon American culture, see the historical evolution of blacks and our achievements. If only there were a way to *show* you, not merely tell you, the whole story of how the race changed the country and the country changed the race. The terrible burden I carry as a collector is the belief that I have this answer in my hands, welling up inside me, and no way to get it out, no way to display it—like a preacher moved but lacking a church, unable to build his own; like a deejay desperate to once again get on the mike but unable to find one.

The best I can do is to build my museum on paper—right here, now, on the few pages that remain.

Take your imagination and touch my heart. Walk through the museum of my mind. See and hear the ghosts come alive as I call the roll. Imagine the audio-visual technology that allows holographic images to burst forth and tell their stories, where the ghosts become the narrators, where hundreds of them, most lost in the crush of time, have their moments in the sun.

Look!

Over there!

Here they come.

With quiet dignity, they introduce themselves . . .

My name is Thomas Rutling. My mother's owner left me motherless by selling her when I was three years old. She held me fast in her arms as if determined to take me with her and did not put me down until the man who had bought her began to beat her with his buggy whip, which wrapped around both mother and child in such an impetuous manner as to have made me feel deeply the strokes and to hear, through all these years, her sobs. But I made my way, eventually, to a new black college in Tennessee, Fisk University, and joined the Fisk Jubilee Singers, and became part of a legendary tour of Europe in the 1870s that raised money needed to keep the young university alive. You have here, before you, my autobiography, *Tom,* which I wrote in London, where I decided to stay rather than return to America.

Here is the booklet we passed out when we performed in Europe under the auspices of the American Missionary Association—the booklet which explained to audiences that seven of the nine singers, including myself, were slaves freed a decade earlier by the Emancipation Proclamation, the booklet which for the first time put down on paper the words and notes of Negro spirituals, the booklet that boasted how, "by the severe discipline to which the Jubilee Singers have been subjected in the schoolroom, they have been educated out of the peculiarities of the Negro dialect, and they do not attempt to imitate the peculiar pronunciation of their race."

Come now, listen to our music and sing "Turn back Pharaoh's Army" with me. (The lyrics will appear on the screen over my shoulder.) Raise your voices for the Lord!

> *Gwine to write Massa Jesus to send some valiant soldier*
> *To turn back Pharaoh's army, ha-luuu*
> *To turn back Pharaoh's army, ha-le-lu-jah*
> *When the children were in bondage, they cried unto the Lord*
> *Turn back Pharaoh's army*
> *He turned back Pharaoh's army . . .*

My name is Anthony Burns, and I offer you this chance to put yourself in my shoes by reading the rare pre–Civil War narrative of my journey, my capture, and the incredible outrage it spawned. Imagine: I was a slave, escaped from Virginia by ship, in the employ of a clothing dealer in Boston when I was arrested in 1854 as a fugitive slave under draconian laws that allowed my owner to reclaim me. Abolitionists forced a public meeting, freed slaves rioted on my behalf, a tense federal trial was held, and the entire soul of New England seemed to be hanging in the balance. The law prevailed: I was returned to slavery under the ownership of Master Suttle in Virginia. As a man who could barely read, it was beyond my ken that *The Boston Slave Riot and Trial of Anthony Burns* would be compiled, presenting in a single volume the trial testimony, newspaper articles, and a detailed account of the events that contributed to the mounting hatred of slavery and ratcheted the fever that made the Civil War inevitable . . .

My name is the Reverend William J. Simmons. In a time when communication was sparse, when it was difficult for Negroes of one county, let alone one state, to communicate with one another, I felt the need to celebrate what the first two decades of freedom had brought our people. In 1887 I compiled and published a 1,141-page book that profiled the achievements of 177 prestigious Negroes in the United States. *Men of Mark: Eminent, Progressive and Rising* could not be sold in stores; it was sold by mail order. I wanted these heroes, many like myself born into slavery, to be exalted. I wanted to snatch their lives from obscurity. One of the few remaining volumes lies in this museum, allowing you to read about not only Frederick Douglass and Crispus Attucks but men like the Reverend James W. Hood, who founded 600 African Methodist Episcopal churches in North and South Carolina and Virginia and supervised the construction of 500 church buildings; Grandville T. Woods, a marine engineer and the inventor of a telegraph system for communicating with moving locomotive trains; the Reverend Nicholas Franklin Roberts, a professor of mathematics and the president of the hundred-thousand-member Baptist State Convention of North Carolina; J. E. Jones, a professor of Greek, born when the State of Virginia prohibited anyone from teaching Negroes to read or write and furtively instructed by a tutor on Sundays between 10 A.M. and noon, when his mother knew white people were usually in church; and Wiley Jones, the owner of a streetcar railroad, a racetrack, and a park—a capitalist worth the staggering sum of 125,000 dollars. So many others, too—violinists, school principals, playwrights, congressmen, historians, lawyers, linguists, colonels, editors—all of them rising, moving toward a destination unthinkable a few years before . . .

My name is William Still, and I kept the records of all the slaves who escaped through the Underground Railroad and made safe passage to Philadelphia. You can read the details in my 780-page book *The Underground Railroad: A Record of Facts, Authentic Narratives, Letters, Etc.,* published in 1872, when it was finally safe to reveal the story. I, like so many others, had much to lose: I was a free black man, a coal dealer in Philadelphia, the owner of Liberty Hall, the largest colored-owned hall in the United States . . .

My name is "Blind Tom" Bethune, one of the most astounding musical geniuses of my day. I was born blind in 1846 to the child of a slave woman in Georgia. My unaccountable gift for the piano and my ability to compose songs at a very young age inspired my owner, Colonel Bethune, to send me on a concert tour and make a fortune for him. I played for President Buchanan at age fourteen. I memorized more than five thousand songs. I could play two different tunes at the same time while singing a third. One night I sat and listened to sixteen compositions by Verdi, Bach, Beethoven, and other great composers and then repeated them in succession on my piano without a single mistake. Here are my testimonials—an article in *Harper's Weekly* in 1866, another in *Ladies' Home Journal,* 1898, a booklet of my songs, and one of my handbills . . .

My name is Thomas Garrett, and on seeing my image you will ask: "What is a white man doing in a black museum?" And my answer, of course, is that this is a *history* museum. I was a Quaker from Delaware, one of the most successful agents on the Underground Railroad, and for this moment I am a living reminder that without white abolitionists, there would have been no Underground Railroad. I am reminded of another white brother, Calvin Fairbanks, who spent eighteen years in a Kentucky prison for the crime of hiding fugitive slaves along the Ohio River and estimated he endured 35,000 strikes on his bare body. Listen to his recollection: "I was flogged bent over a chair, often receiving seventy blows four times a day . . . , particles of flesh striking the wall several feet away." They caught me, too, and convicted me, and fined me so heavily that I lost all my property and was penniless at age sixty. When the auctioneer finished selling my last piece, he said to me: "I hope you will never be guilty of doing the like again." I looked at him. "Friend," I said, "I have not a dollar in the world, but if thee knows a fugitive slave who needs breakfast, send him to me." My story, and Mister Fairbanks's story, were lost to the ages, but they come alive in a 1898 book, *Progress of a Race: The Remarkable Advancement of the American Negro,* written by two Negroes who did not forget, H. F. Kletzing and W. H. Crogman . . .

My name is Denmark Veazie. I was born in the Virgin Islands and purchased as a slave at fourteen. I became a carpenter and bought my freedom, and then I became inspired. As you can read in my trial testimony, I formed a plan two decades later to liberate the slaves of Charleston, South Carolina—and was hung, along with fourteen of my compatriots . . .

My name is Richard B. Harrison, and during the unlikeliest of times I was God. I was the son of a fugitive slave and worked as a farmhand, bellboy, waiter, Pullman porter, police clerk, reader, lecturer, and teacher. For three decades I entertained colored audiences with one-man performances of *Macbeth* and *Julius Caesar.* Then a white man named Marc Connelly wrote one of the finest plays about Negro life, *The Green Pastures.* It made the rounds of Broadway houses, but many stage managers refused it on the grounds that it would be impossible to cast the central part, "De Lawd," without seeming sacrilegious. It was 1929, and I was teaching drama at North Carolina A&T when they found me, and 1,656 times I played God on Broadway. Later Hollywood made *The Green Pastures* into a movie, and the great Hall Johnson, who composed the score out of Negro spirituals, called the story "the finest dramatic expression of the spirit that imbues those songs, the spirit of proud humility, of unswerving determination, of unalterable love . . ."

My name is Phillis Wheatley. You know me as the second woman in America to publish a book, but how much else do you know? Do you know what it means to witness an original printing of my first book, published in 1773? Did you know I was not an African American but an African? John Wheatley's wife found me in the Boston slave market in 1761 and bought me, at age seven or eight, but instead of making me a servant, she noticed my intelligence and taught me to read. After only a year and a half in America, I could easily read difficult parts of the Bible. The literary people of Boston supported me, and when I was nineteen, a 120-page book of my poems was published in London. Read along with me now, and think about the implausibility of my journey:

> *Great God, incomprehensible, unknown*
> *By sense, we bow at thine exalted throne.*
> *O, while we beg thine excellence to feel*
> *Thy sacred Spirit to our hearts reveal,*
> *And give us of that mercy to partake,*
> *Which thou hast promis'd for the Savior's sake . . .*

My name is Mammy Ellen Pleasant, the "Voodoo Queen." I was born a slave, sold for $600 at an early age, and sent to New Orleans, where I practiced a voodoo ritual my mother had taught me, helped many slaves escape to the North, and aided John Brown. After the Civil War I headed to San Francisco, where I wielded a strange and sinister influence over some of the city's leading citizens for more than half a century. Many people swore I lived to help my people; others whispered that the blood of more than one man was on my hands. Here are my canceled checks, reminders of a time when truth and lore were dangerously entwined . . .

My name is George Henderson. I founded Henderson Business College in January 1912 with $2.20 and two used typewriters to my name. Two years later I devised a system of shorthand and created a correspondence school in Nashville with the money I made selling the system. Many short-sighted farmers said, "That fellow Henderson must be losing his mind. Doesn't he know he's spoiling some mighty good fieldhands? Who's going to hire colored bookkeepers and stenographers?" They learned. I bet you never knew that I was the man who coined two phrases you probably heard in school: "He profits most who serves the best" and "Great oaks from little acorns grow . . ."

My name is Robert Blair. I invented a gun. I am no hoodlum. The gun I invented was the antiaircraft gun . . .

My name is Lt. Col. T. W. Higginson, a white man who was so taken by the colored soldiers I commanded during the Civil War that I wrote *Army Life in a Black Regiment,* published in 1862. I documented the First South Carolina Volunteers, a regiment formed before the Fifty-fourth Massachusetts regiment that was later made famous by the popular film *Glory.* Listen while I read a passage from Christmas Day 1861: "*'We'll fight for liberty 'till de Lord shall call us home.'* This is the hymn which the slaves at Georgetown, South Carolina, were whipped for singing when Lincoln was elected. So said a little drummer boy as he sat at my tent's edge last night. 'Dey think de Lord meant for say *de Yankees,'* he said . . ."

My name is Annie M. Pope Turnbo-Malone. I studied chemistry and began manufacturing hair-growing products in 1900 in Illinois. I broke ground for Poro College in 1917. As you can read in this 1922 brochure, Poro College was consecrated to the uplift of humanity—race women in particular. At one point I had 75,000 women selling my products . . .

My name is Oscar Micheaux. When I started my all-black film company in the 1920s, it was viewed as a preposterous notion because, among other things, there were no places to show my films. I would have to use churches or private organizations or get a theater to let me run it on one night, for colored only. I didn't need Hollywood. I worked outside it with my own "sepia" casts in New York, and I churned out hits in the thirties and forties: *Lem Hawkins' Confession, The Betrayal* (based on the novel *The Wind from Nowhere*), and *Midnight Menace* (a film about voodoo).

I want you to think about the audacity of what I did in an era in which we were allowed to play nothing but maids. Look around you. This museum has dozens of my lobby cards and the films themselves. It also has a priceless snippet of film—the only such trace remaining—made by the Lincoln Motion Picture Company, which preceded me by a good ten years. Lincoln, the first Negro movie company, operated during the era of silent pictures. Its lobby cards and incorporation papers are here, too . . .

My name is Montague. Imagine these ghosts, and so many others whose work I have captured, introducing themselves to you. Imagine being caught up in the swirl. Imagine hearing voice after voice: Black Herman, our own Houdini, who barnstormed the nation and wrote a book about his bag of tricks, like how to burn a handkerchief with your own breath; Peter Jackson, the great scientific boxer who went sixty rounds in a no-decision bout with James J. Corbett in 1891; the X-ray specialist and Harlem Renaissance author Rudolph Fisher; William Whipper, who ran a successful lumberyard in Pennsylvania, used his own funds to help runaway slaves, and delivered an address on nonviolent resistance a dozen years before Thoreau wrote his famous essay on civil disobedience; Charles Stewart, a jockey who told his life story to his nephew in an 1884 *Harper's* magazine article rendered entirely in Stewart's dialect; Bill Pickett, the cowboy movie star and originator of the art of bulldogging—the technique of leaping from his horse and grabbing the steer around his neck; E. Simms Campbell, the famed early illustrator for *Esquire* (fabled alone for a stunning cover of the Negro journal *Opportunity* showing a black boy looking at a chicken in a window, a small sign showing fifty-one as the winning lottery number, and the boy holding a ticket with the number fifty on it); Elizabeth Keckly, who bought herself out of slavery by her skill as a seamstress and became Mary Todd Lincoln's White House dressmaker and confidante; the folk art collection of Sister Gertrude Morgan, who began painting exuberant biblical-themed watercolors in old age and who sang and played guitar on twenty of her songs when I went to her home in New Orleans to taperecord her in 1970; Grafton Tyler Brown, one of the West's most noted landscape artists in the late nineteenth century . . .

Oh, and the art! The hand-colored engravings and drawings— look! Look at this set, drawn in Africa in the 1840s, the black soldiers and Africans, warriors and nobility, bushmen—the sharpness of the images, the hand-drawn detail that demands your attention, so much more revealing than the photographic images that would follow twenty years hence; a priceless oil painting on canvas of a young slave couple, captioned *He Lubs Me, He Lubs Me*

Not; a huge poster of the movie *St. Louis Blues* starring Bessie Smith, queen of the blues (and of course the 35-millimeter print itself); turn-of-the-century postcards painting their laughable caricatures: a black infant stalked by a crocodile with "Little African" across the top and "A Dainty Morsel" across the bottom; a little pamphlet based on the character Topsy from *Uncle Tom's Cabin,* with verse and pictures inside casually stating: "There was a little nigger girl, with face as black as coal, and many little wooly curls she grew upon her poll . . ."

And right around the corner, book after book and document after document filled with courageous prescience in the face of such derision: an 1804 booklet containing all the speeches of the American Convention for Promoting the Abolition of Slavery and Improving the Condition of the African Race, so old that the *S*s resemble *F*s, advising free black men that if they "place a proper estimate on your privileges, and act in a manner becoming your character . . . , you may destroy the prejudices which some persons entertain against you"; flashing ahead eighty-seven years to hear Edward Johnson, a North Carolina school principal, predict in 1891: "Some time in the next 50 years the historians of American affairs will be confronted with the world miracle of that day: a black man from whom has been eliminated everything save color that once set him apart from his Anglo Saxon neighbor as an inferior type of humanity"; continuing the journey eleven more years and listening to the Reverend H. A. Monroe of Philadelphia foreseeing: "A warm-blooded, tropical child of nature, the Negro will yet give to America some of its very choicest treasures of art and song . . ."

And then, ruefully, back it up a decade for the Negro playwright William Edgar Easton, who said in the preface to his 1893 play about Haitian ruler Dessalines: "The Negro alone fails to immortalize his distinguished dead and leaves to the prejudiced pen of other races the office which, by a proper conception of duty to posterity, very properly becomes his duty."

I have tried to do my duty.

I have tried to raise these ghosts, parade them before you, shine the light of revelation upon them, sing their praises. I have strained to make them come to life, sitting as they do now in cardboard boxes, thousands of pieces, a couple hundred beginning to fall prey to the ravages of rodents, reminding me again that it is time to move on, time to divest myself of this collection. I can do this, but promise me that as you close this book you will take a shard of my collection with you.

Promise me you will tell someone else some of these great stories so they know—and so that you remember—what great deeds can be performed in the face of impossible odds.

Tell them so that they understand that nothing is impossible, that you can live your dreams, and that you should always have a dream.

Oh, I can hear you now. I can especially hear the young people, the ones who have less than they'd like, less than they need: "*You* had a dream, old man, and look at it—it died. Whassup with that?"

And the answer, I believe, is that I've seen the alternative to dreaming. I've seen it all around me, all my life. I've seen where being afraid of being called cocky gets you. I've seen where taking only what you're given and not striving for more gets you. And I'd rather have failed than not tried.

Remember Howard Cosell, that pompous sportscaster on TV? One time he was interviewing a fighter nicknamed the Jewish Bomber after a victory, and Howard intoned like a know-it-all: "You know, after your previous fight ended in defeat—"

And the Jewish Bomber stopped him.

"Howard, that was not a *defeat,*" he said matter-of-factly. "It was a *lesson.*"

I cherish every lesson life has taught me, and I'm determined not to go out feeling sorry for myself. Ultimately, my exhibits will live; they simply will not live with me. If I've sparked the inquirer in you, a desire to go deeper, it was worth it. If I've made you think about visiting a museum or some historical site on your next vacation, it was worth it. If I've given you new eyes for lost souls, it was worth it.

Because, through you, and through what I'm passing down, I will live forever. Ultimately, that's bigger than any building. What happens to my collection is up to those who have the wherewithal to purchase and preserve it. It's time for me to lower my voice. Like we say in the recording studio when the singer comes to the end of the last verse, fade me on the board.

Fade the voice, baby.
Let that music play.
Burn, baby! Burn!
And learn, baby . . . learn.

Index

Abner, Ewart, 67

Ace, Johnny, 40, 42, 43

Advertising: portrayal of African Americans in, 146–47; radio, 41–42, 64–67

African, The, 147

African Americans: in advertising, 146–47; and Africa, 24–26, 180–81; art, 147, 148–49, 180–81; "blue-vein," 78; and the civil rights movement, 61, 74–76, 90; culture of, 59–61, 72–73, 171–73, 181–83; as deejays, 7–8, 9, 28, 55, 57–58, 77–79, 90; influence on music, 32–34, 59, 62, 70–72, 92–93, 113–14, 137–38, 176; and interracial marriages, 49–50, 145; and Jews, 82–84; and magazines, 78, 87–88; memorabilia, 3–4, 5, 6–11, 79, 86–88, 101, 102, 117–18, 146–49, 166, 168; in the Merchant Marine, 20–21, 28, 31, 35; migration of, to Chicago, 54–55; migration of, to the north, 17; migration of, to the west, 18; in the military, 23–24; and motion pictures, 10, 14, 179; and music companies, 42–43, 55–56, 59, 64, 67–69, 93–94, 99–101, 113, 115, 119–20, 120, 121–22, 149–52; and the Nation of Islam, 30–31, 96–98; as performers, 32–34, 42, 59, 89–90, 92–95, 107–8, 110–22, 148, 179, 180–81; poetry by, 51–53, 58–59, 72–73, 78–79, 116–17, 178; as radio market, 29; and religion, 14–15, 38, 80, 107; segregation of, 13, 14, 22–23, 31–32, 56, 75, 83, 86–87, 125–26, 145–46; and slavery, 8, 9, 10, 17–18, 52, 60–61, 103–9, 118, 132, 173–79, 181; and the Watts riots, 1–2, 9, 123–35, 166; writings by, 52, 76, 97, 98, 103–9, 148–49, 173–82

Aladdin Records, 82

American Bandstand, 70

American Convention for Promoting the Abolition of Slavery, 181

American Federation of Radio Artists, 34

American Graffiti, 150

American Guild of Musical Artists, 34

American Missionary Association, 174

Amos, Wally, 153

Anderson, Eddie, 2

Anderson, Marian, 10

Andrews Sisters, 165

Anti-Semitism, 17, 30

Apartheid, 24

Armstrong, Louis, 33

Army Life in a Black Regiment, 179

Arrington, Barbara, 69

Art, African American, 147, 148–49, 180–81

Atlantic Records, 82, 83, 91, 120

Attucks, Crispus, 175

Axton, Estelle, 140

Axton, Packy, 140

MAGNIFICENT MONTAGUE is one of America's preeminent collectors of African American memorabilia as well as a legendary rhythm-and-blues disc jockey. Born in New Jersey, he became R&B radio's most exciting voice on stations in Chicago, New York, Los Angeles, and many other cities in the fifties and sixties. His fiery slogan at Los Angeles's KGFJ—"Burn, baby! Burn!"—inadvertently became the anthem of the Watts riots in 1965. Montague and his wife, Rose Catalon, live in Las Vegas.

BOB BAKER, who heard Montague on the air in 1965 as a teenaged fan, has been a reporter, an editor, and a writing coach for thirty-three years, the past twenty-five at the *Los Angeles Times,* where he now covers popular culture. He is the author of *Newsthinking* (Allyn and Bacon, 2002), a book on mental organization for journalists, and operates a Web site, www.newsthinking.com. He lives in Los Angeles with his wife, Marjorie, and their daughter, Amanda.

Music in American Life